Essential Histories

The Suez Crisis 1956

Essential Histories

The Suez Crisis 1956

Derek Varble

OSPREY
PUBLISHING

First published in Great Britain in 2003 by Osprey Publishing,
Elms Court, Chapel Way, Botley, Oxford OX2 9LP
Email: info@ospreypublishing.com

ISBN 1 84176 418 3

A CIP catalogue record for this book is available from the British
Library

Editor: Sally Rawlings

Design: Ken Vail Graphic Design, Cambridge, UK
Cartography by The Map Studio
Index by Susan Williams
Picture research by Image Select International
Origination by Grasmere Digital Imaging, Leeds, UK
Printed and bound in China by L. Rex Printing Company Ltd.

03 04 05 06 07   10 9 8 7 6 5 4 3 2 1

For a complete list of titles available from Osprey Publishing
please contact:

Osprey Direct UK, PO Box 140,
Wellingborough, Northants, NN8 2FA, UK.
Email: info@ospreydirect.co.uk

Osprey Direct USA, c/o MBI Publishing,
PO Box 1, 729 Prospect Ave,
Osceola, WI 54020, USA.
Email: info@ospreydirectusa.com

www.ospreypublishing.com

Acknowledgements
My wife Amy is the sunlight in my universe and made this
project possible. Amy's grace, warmth, and humor always inspire
me. She suffered as a "book widow" for far too long. Thanks also
to my family: Elizabeth, Dale, Charles, Mary Ellen, Steve, Emily,
Dave, Ann, Sarah, Kathy, Caleb, and Leah. Spending time with
them enriches my life.

Dr Robert O'Neill is a scholar and gentleman representing the
finest academic and professional traditions. Bob played a key role
in the origin and development of this project. His wisdom and
insight have been a tremendous benefit not only in terms of the
book but in a broader sense as well. Bob is a true mentor, and I
am fortunate to profit from his example.

Jason McInerney and Scott Hebbeler generously donated their
time to read part or all of this manuscript. Both made many
useful suggestions regarding content, grammar, and style.

The staff at Osprey Publishing showed kindness and patience in
bringing this project to fruition. Their assistance transformed my
freewheeling prose into a tighter, more organized narrative. Our
collaboration has, I think, resulted in a volume that at the very
least provides a summary of a complex, fascinating historical era.

Responsibility for mistakes or omissions in this manuscript is
mine alone.

Contents

Introduction

In July 1956 Egypt nationalized the Suez Canal and triggered a crisis. Despite extensive diplomacy, war soon resulted. Britain and France joined Israel in a coalition against Egypt; their goals included capturing Sinai and the Suez Canal and toppling the Egyptian government. Before striking, the three nations synchronized their attacks: Israel started the conflict and France and Britain joined two days later.

Israel invaded Egypt on 29 October. Israeli paratroops attacked Mitla Pass in western Sinai, with an overland column joining them a day later. After fighting local Egyptian

Infantry departing Britain for occupation duty in Egypt, November 1956. These and other British and French occupation forces withdrew from Egypt the following month. (Topham Picturepoint)

formations, the paratroops advanced into southern Sinai, assisting in the capture of Sharm el-Sheikh, the gateway to the Tiran Straits, thereby relieving the Egyptian blockade of this passage. Israel also attacked northern and central Sinai, where armor and night operations secured an Israeli victory. In the north, Israeli forces encircled key outposts, allowing the subsequent conquest of al-Arish and Gaza. In the central zone, the fortunes of war ebbed and flowed for three days at Egypt's frontier fortifications. Israeli tanks pressured these points on several fronts, forcing their abandonment. Israeli forces subsequently advanced across Sinai, attaining all their goals.

Egypt was then in retreat. British and French bombardment triggered this withdrawal, which Egyptian President Gamal Abdel Nasser directed in order to avoid a trap. Nasser correctly thought that the aerial onslaught heralded a British and French invasion: after bombing Egypt for over 100 hours, Britain and France committed ground forces to the war. On 5 November, paratroops from both nations attacked the northern Suez Canal Zone, capturing some but not all of Port Said. One day later a marine and armored force entered the battle, fighting several urban skirmishes against Egyptian irregulars. That night, November 6, reinforcements – some arriving via helicopter – reached the outskirts of al-Qantarah, 40 km (25 miles) south of Port Said, where a UN ceasefire halted their progress. Britain and France stopped their Egyptian operations because of overwhelming international pressure.

Political developments also ultimately reversed British, French, and Israeli military accomplishments. The United States compelled Britain and France to leave Egypt, and Israel to withdraw from Sinai. In November 1956, UN peacekeepers arrived in the Canal Zone, soon replacing British and French forces there. Four months later, a similar transition occurred in Sinai, where Israel yielded to international troops. Egyptian boundaries reverted to their pre-war configuration, and Nasser retained his hold on power and the Suez Canal.

On the road to al-Qantarah: a British Buffalo tank and troops of 3 Commando Brigade assaulting Port Said by sea. (Topham Picturepoint)

Chronology

1948

14 May Israel's creation

15 May First Arab–Israeli War erupts

1949

31 January Israel and Egypt sign armistice ending First Arab–Israeli War

1952

23 July Revolutionary Command Council replaces King Farouk in Egypt

1953

January Dwight D. Eisenhower becomes president of the United States

1954

July Signing of Anglo-Egyptian Treaty ending British occupation of Egypt

1955

28 February Israel raids Gaza

April Anthony Eden becomes British prime minister

September Egypt tightens blockade of Tiran Straits

Egypt announces arms deal with Czechoslovakia

December Israeli Chief of Staff recommends attacking Sinai

Unsuccessful British attempt to bring Jordan into Baghdad Pact

1956

1 March Hussein of Jordan removes General John Glubb as Arab Legion chief

March United States and Britain launch plan to weaken Egypt

19 July United States announces no American funding for Aswan Dam

26 July Egypt nationalizes Suez Canal

10 August Britain and France plan to capture Alexandria; advance on Cairo

11 August General Charles Keightley designated Supreme Allied Commander

9 September Britain and France change emphasis: Musketeer becomes Revise

5 October Israel develops a plan (Kadesh) for Sinai conquest

22–24 October Sevres meetings: Israel, France, and Britain plan their Egyptian campaign

24 October Israel mobilizes reserves

25 October Israel revises Kadesh, in keeping with Sevres meetings

26 October Israel begins emergency mobilization

Carriers *Bulwark*, *Eagle*, and *Arromanches* leave Malta

29 October Israeli forces attack Mitla Pass

Israeli forces capture Ras an-Naqb

30 October Israeli forces capture al-Qusaymah

Israeli forces repulsed at Umm Shihan

Britain demands Israel and Egypt withdraw 16km (10 miles) from Suez Canal

Israeli forces reach west flank of Ruafa

Israeli forces rendezvous near Mitla Pass

31 October Anglo-French ultimatum expires

Israeli forces capture Jebel Heitan and Ruafa

British and French warplanes bomb Egyptian airfields

Royal Marines leave Malta aboard Royal Navy Landing Ships Tank

1 November Britain and France destroy Egyptian air force; gain air superiority

Israel captures Umm Shihan
and Umm Qataf
UN General Assembly votes for
immediate Middle Eastern
ceasefire

2 November Israeli forces capture Gaza City,
northern half of Gaza Strip,
and Tor

3 November British warplanes strike
Egyptian transmitters,
disabling Radio Cairo
Israel completes conquest of
Gaza Strip
Royal Marines leave Malta
aboard *Ocean* and *Theseus*

4 November French warplanes destroy
Egyptian bombers at Luxor

5 November Israel captures Sharm el-
Sheikh; Sinai campaign ends
British and French paratroops
enter Port Said; capture Gamil
and Raswa
British and French armada
reaches Egyptian coast

6 November British marines capture Port
Said via amphibious assault
Britain and France agree to UN
ceasefire
Lead British elements halt at
al-Tinah; resume advance soon
after
Eisenhower re-elected as
president

7 November Ceasefire takes effect in Egypt
British and French forces halt
at al-Cap, north of al-Qantarah

23 November Eden leaves Britain for Jamaica

3 December Britain announces imminent
withdrawal of forces from Egypt

17 December Eden makes first speech since
leaving for Jamaica several
weeks before

22 December Last Anglo-French troops leave
Egypt

1957
9 January Eden resigns as prime minister
March Israel completes withdrawal
from Sinai

The Suez Crisis and its military implications

The Suez Canal in historical context

In 1869 workers linked the Mediterranean and Red Seas by completing a waterway across an isthmus at the junction of Africa and Asia. Since its southern end adjoined the Gulf of Suez, this passage became known as the Suez Canal. Successful construction of such a vast engineering project depended on abundant native labor, Frenchman Ferdinand de Lesseps's entrepreneurial efforts, and plentiful Egyptian and European capital.

The Canal's revolutionary advantages immediately became apparent. Existing trade routes and supply lines between Europe and Asia stretched around the coast of southern Africa. The Suez Canal, however, shortened these maritime paths by thousands of miles while avoiding the southern ocean's dangerous weather. Suez soon became an imperial lifeline: it increased efficiency while offering new economic opportunities to Britain's far-flung empire. When the British government changed the Royal Navy's fuel from coal to oil in 1912, the Suez Canal became of truly vital importance to Britain's home security.

In the decades after the Canal's completion, therefore, British leaders made a priority of acquiring shares in the Suez Canal Company, a French-based consortium responsible for Canal operations and maintenance. By the 1880s, when a series of treaties codified the Canal's "international" status, Britain had a controlling interest in the waterway. At the same time, British leaders pursued an aggressive geopolitical strategy to avoid any interruption of Canal traffic.

To preclude such a contingency, Britain deployed an expeditionary army to Alexandria in 1882. The subsequent occupation, which lasted 74 years and forced Egypt into vassalage, perpetuated British control of the Canal. But strategic success carried a political price. Egyptian independence societies, many espousing anti-British attitudes, proliferated and often instigated riots. These disturbances often flared up at what for Britain were singularly inopportune moments, such as the 20th-century world wars. The 1956 Suez Crisis is often portrayed as the climax of Egypt's decades-long struggle to cast off British domination.

Other forces besides Egyptian discord also threatened Britain's passage to India. In November 1914, the Ottoman Empire decided to join the Central Powers against Britain and its Triple Entente allies. Eight years earlier, Britain obtained Sinai from the Ottoman Turks. However, this acquisition provided the Canal with an inadequate eastern buffer, as became clear in February 1915 when Turkish and German forces in Palestine stormed west to Suez.

Although these efforts failed to capture or close the Canal, the shock of nearly losing such an important asset led British leaders to expand their army of Egyptian occupation to 100,000 troops for the remainder of World War I. To ease the threat facing Britain's control of Suez, an Egyptian Expeditionary Force, successively under the command of Generals Archibald Murray and Edmund Allenby, battered across Sinai. By late 1918 not only had Allenby re-established the Canal's peninsular buffer, but had delivered a deathblow to the Ottoman Empire.

Twenty years later, events again thrust the Suez Canal into the forefront of global conflict. Hitler understood the waterway's importance to British imperial strategy, and knew that cutting this lifeline would isolate Britain from its overseas possessions and allies. After World War II began, Germany therefore attempted to block or even capture the Canal. Its first attempt occurred in March 1941, when Luftwaffe bombers mined Suez, stopping all maritime traffic for several days.

This aerial strike, while impressive, failed to satisfy Hitler's fixation with fracturing the British Empire. In 1942 he directed two armored pincers to converge on the Canal, one from the North African desert and another from the Caucasus. Field Marshal Erwin Rommel, commanding the western force, in 1942 advanced as far as Alamein, where German logistics faltered, ending the danger from western Egypt. In the Caucasus, various Soviet distractions preoccupied the Wehrmacht, preventing a Nazi drive on Egypt from the north.

Thus throughout World War II Britain retained possession of the Canal, a key aspect of victory over the Axis. During the course of the war an influx of Allied troops flooded military bases adjoining Suez. These installations became some of the world's largest in terms of manpower and logistics infrastructure, making the area a linchpin of British imperial strength.

After the war, the breakup of the British Empire, in particular India's independence in 1947, diminished the traditional significance of the Suez Canal as Britain's conduit to South and East Asia. However, in the 20th century navies and industrial economies became oil-based rather than coal-based. Britain's economic recovery after World War II thus required an abundance of affordable petroleum. Without this strategic resource, Britain's "Great Power" status might end.

The most important British source for this commodity was the Middle East, especially Iran, Iraq, Kuwait, and the Persian Gulf sultanate that later became Oman and the United Arab Emirates. Various pipelines transferred oil from these areas to Mediterranean ports for conveyance to Britain. Since these overland routes were susceptible to Middle Eastern chaos, such as Syrian instability and the 1948 creation of Israel, British leaders preferred an all-sea route for petroleum transport.

By far the shortest such path passed through Suez, arising in the Persian Gulf and running to the Atlantic via the Mediterranean and Arabian Seas. By the 1950s, two-thirds of Britain's entire oil supply – over 20 million tons annually – traveled this route. Limited tanker capacity meant that the alternative sea route – the circumnavigation of southern Africa – was insufficient to meet domestic British demand.

It was in this context that Egypt took control of the Suez Canal in 1956. British petroleum dependence provided powerful motivation to respond, even with drastic measures such as the ousting of President Nasser. As outlined elsewhere in this book, Britain had other reasons for opposing Nasser – his opposition to pro-British Hashemite dynasts, for example – but the Suez Canal's role as a key oil conduit figured largely in Eden's decision to use force against Egypt.

Ironically, the Suez Canal's five-month closure during 1956–57 precipitated a long-term transition to the southern African shipping route. By the late 20th century, only a small fraction of Middle East petroleum passed through the Canal. This development, along with discovery of North Sea oil, rendered the Suez Canal insignificant in British strategy.

Origins of the crisis

The 1956 Suez–Sinai War sprang from a 23 July 1952 military coup in Egypt. Replacing King Farouk were the Free Officers. Their political arm, the Revolutionary Command Council (RCC), advocated pan-Arab nationalism, which envisaged a single state spanning North Africa, Mesopotamia, and the Arabian Peninsula.

Governments favoring the regional status quo opposed Arab unity under Egyptian auspices. These included Israel, France, and Britain. Israel, fighting with neighboring states since its creation in 1948, favored Arab fragmentation. A 1949 Israeli–Egyptian armistice failed to quell violence along their common boundary. France, facing

The Suez Crisis begins: Nasser leaving Alexandria after nationalising the Suez Canal, 26 July 1956. (Topham Picturepoint)

insurgencies in its North African colonies, saw Egypt as a supplier for Arab rebels and thus opposed Nasser, who in turn openly encouraged an end to European overseas empires and in 1954 consolidated his control of Egypt's government.

That year Britain and Egypt signed a treaty ending the 72-year British military occupation of Egypt, although Anglo-Egyptian relations remained contentious. Britain, particularly Anthony Eden who became prime minister in 1955, feared Nasser because Arab unity threatened a key client, Iraq's Hashemite dynasty. Cheap Iraqi petroleum, vital to Britain's economy, depended on Hashemite rule. Ensuing British subversion of pan-Arab nationalism was multi-faceted, and in each case used its Iraqi client. With limited success, Britain fashioned the Hashemites as an alternative to Nasserite hegemony while working to strengthen Iraq.

One measure, the Turko-Iraqi Pact – interestingly, an American initiative – sought to buttress Iraq's Hashemites by drawing Syria and Jordan closer to Baghdad.

Egypt, Saudi Arabia, and Syria all opposed an accretion of Hashemite strength. They subsequently formed a rival organization, thus splitting the Arab world into rival blocs. Hostility intensified as each coalition sought additional membership. Britain's 1955 attempt to persuade Jordan to join Iraq precipitated serious violence, nearly caused Jordan's dissolution, and convinced British leaders that Nasser must go. Apparent Egyptian complicity in Arab Legion commander John Bagot Glubb's dismissal a few months later increased British anger towards Nasser.

Heightened Arab–Israeli conflict accompanied the upsurge in inter-Arab tensions. In 1955 attacks increased across the 1949 armistice lines. *Fedayeen* (partisans) from Gaza, Egypt, Jordan, and Syria struck towns and settlements in Israel, while Israeli commandos attacked Arab outposts.

Prominent among these incursions was Operation Black Arrow, Israel's Gaza raid of early 1955. In response, Egypt tightened its Tiran Straits blockade. This barrier, in place since 1953, denied Israel access to the Red Sea. Nasser also concluded an arms deal with Czechoslovakia in which Egypt received advanced Soviet weaponry, including armor, artillery, and jet warplanes. David Ben-Gurion, a founder of Israel who became prime minister in November 1955, thought these actions threatened Israel's survival.

Nasser's Soviet dalliance also angered Washington. In 1956, American and British leaders began Omega, a plan for regime change in Egypt. Consistent with Omega, on 14 July 1956 Secretary of State John Foster Dulles informed Egyptian Ambassador Ahmed Hussein of the United States' decision not to fund a dam along the Nile at Aswan. Nasser reacted by nationalizing the Suez Canal during anniversary celebrations of the 1952 coup. This action ended the Paris-based Suez Canal Company's concession for Canal control. Outraged shareholders included Britain and France, which decided to overthrow Nasser. The Suez Crisis was on.

Diversity in capabilities, doctrine, and leadership

Britain

Britain emerged from World War II with formidable military forces. These withered through the next decade as fiscal crises and economic malaise exacted a toll in key areas such as readiness, reach, and technology.

Despite overall deterioration, the 16th Independent Parachute Brigade Group remained a key British asset for projecting power to distant theaters such as Egypt. However, this elite unit had training and equipment limitations that iron discipline and high morale could not transcend. The Cyprus emergency had largely transformed the brigade into a rural counterinsurgency force, fighting primarily on the ground against the EOKA independence movement. Many in the brigade thus lacked current training in the skills that would have distinguished them from other military forces: jumping from airplanes into enemy territory. Brigade operations against EOKA guerrillas also contributed to the neglect of equipment specific to airborne operations rather than generalized ground combat.

The Royal Navy, an area of traditional British prowess, could project power some

EOKA rebels. As operations in Cyprus against George Grivas and his EOKA insurgents kept 16th Independent Parachute Brigade from training, the unit was unprepared to parachute into Egypt at the outset of the Suez Crisis. (Topham Picturepoint)

distance inland using aircraft carriers (naval aviation) and battleships (gunnery). Amphibious strength, however, proved lacking in 1956. Littoral capabilities were particularly important because attacking from the sea was Britain's only realistic invasion route into Egypt. Armored, tracked landing craft were particularly scarce. These vessels, which propelled and protected troops as they assaulted defended beaches, were critical to a successful invasion.

Recent Royal Air Force (RAF) additions were two long-range bombers, the twin-turbojet English Electric Canberra, and the four-turbojet swept-wing Vickers Valiant, the first of Britain's "V bombers." These warplanes could carry either nuclear or large conventional payloads, the latter more appropriate for the Suez Crisis. The newness of the Canberras and Valiants meant that the RAF had yet to establish effective bombing techniques, especially in the unfamiliar Middle Eastern landscape where radar beacons and other targeting aids were absent. Night sorties, which constituted the bulk of British bomber operations during the Suez Crisis, further diminished accuracy since darkness forced crews to rely on instrumentation rather than on visual clues.

Nonetheless General Charles Keightley, commander-in-chief of British and French forces during the Suez Crisis, thought such bombers alone could attain victory. This assumption owed much to Keightley's belief in technological and doctrinal innovation, combined with his feeling that air power represented a politically inexpensive path to victory.

Whereas Keightley favored strategic bombing, his subordinate, General Hugh Stockwell, Task Force commander for British and French ground forces during the Suez Crisis, preferred more established combat arms such as armor. Stockwell, who gained Middle Eastern experience through his

Generals Hugh Stockwell, Andre Beaufre, and Jacques Massu review and congratulate French paratroops at Port Said. (Topham Picturepoint)

participation in Britain's withdrawal from Palestine a decade earlier, was militarily conservative. He avoided risk where possible and made decisions only after careful analysis of available information.

Stockwell's zest for armor owed in part to Britain's impressive main battle tank, the Centurion. This vehicle, which dated from World War II, weighed 50 tonnes, and its heavy gun and thick armor made it a powerful force in intense combat. These attributes also made it slow and awkward. Port Said's urban setting provided an ideal Centurion environment, whereas the relatively open terrain south of Port Said favored speedier, more agile tanks.

France

The Suez Crisis found the French military over-extended. Since World War II France had campaigned in vain to retain far-flung colonies. Liberation struggles in Southeast Asia and North Africa proved especially burdensome. Dien Bien Phu alone cost thousands of casualties and vast quantities of supplies, although defeat ended France's military commitments in Asia.

This was not the case in Algeria, however, where a protracted war flared anew, pitting Algerian Muslims against European colonists. As each side pursued unlimited objectives – Algeria sought complete independence while France insisted that Algeria was inherently French – the conflict intensified in the mid-1950s. By 1956, tens of thousands of French troops were deployed in North Africa.

Thus the nationalization of the Suez Canal presented France with both a threat and an opportunity. Fighting in Egypt meant diverting resources from Algeria but also provided a chance to destroy Nasser, who supported the Algerian independence movement. Destroying Nasser meant attacking Egypt, and although France had some ability to execute such an operation, in other ways its capabilities were inadequate to the task.

The French navy could execute advanced tasks, such as inland air strikes from carrier-based warplanes, but, like Britain, had limited amphibious capability. This weakness owed more to materiel rather than personnel – French marines had adequate training and personal equipment to assault enemy beaches if suitable landing craft were available. As in the case of Britain, deficiencies in littoral operations meant responsibility for power projection rested primarily with elite French paratroops, including the Foreign Legion and Regiment de Parachutistes Coloniaux (RPC).

A legacy of fierce engagements in Asian jungles and other theaters had sharpened men and equipment to a hard edge while imparting a sense of fatalism that intensified their bravery. These warriors knew how to fight fluid battles against an elusive adversary. Their ruthlessness dictated a "shoot first, ask questions later" code, while their resourcefulness allowed them to campaign for extended periods with minimal logistical support. Into battle French paratroops carried a lean but effective collection of weapons, allowing for both effective fighting and mobility. For example, French paratroops, unlike their British counterparts, could fire their weapons while under canopy, a useful attribute when assaulting enemy territory.

Apart from these elite forces, French ground troops were competent but not outstanding. Since French doctrine emphasized mobility at the expense of shock, tanks such as the AMX-13 were agile but thinly protected and lightly gunned, precisely the opposite of their British armored counterparts. Rather than engaging the enemy's main battle tanks, French commanders preferred campaigns of movement in which encirclement was the main objective.

An architect of this doctrine, General Andre Beaufre, was France's best commander during the Suez Crisis. In his position as Stockwell's deputy, Beaufre articulated a clear, tactically sensible plan for attaining Anglo-French objectives. By contrast, Keightley's deputy, Admiral Pierre Barjot, seemed lost in the political complexity of

French paratroops drifitng to earth in Southeast Asia.
In the foreground is a helmeted para adjusting his gear;
a rifle rests on his pack and in the midground a standing
para looks in the general direction of the camera.
(Topham Picturepoint)

the Suez Crisis. For instance, at every
opportunity Barjot advocated direct Israeli
involvement in French operations,
apparently not realizing that such
participation was merely a means to an end
rather than an end in itself.

Israel

Although in 1956 Israel's armed forces were
the best in the Middle East, various
deficiencies plagued the Israeli Defence Force
(IDF), including immature doctrine, faulty
logistics, and technical inadequacies. Some
of these liabilities had external causes, but
others arose within the IDF itself. Seeking,
like France, to emphasize the use of mobile
forces, chief-of-staff Major General Moshe

Dayan cultivated creativity, initiative, and
offensive spirit in all echelons of the Israeli
leadership. Yet he neglected some essential
components of mobility: logistics and armor.

Most Israeli units depended on a
haphazard supply system for fuel, spares, and
other necessities. Such arrangements sufficed
for border raids and other limited operations,
but lengthy campaigns required a more
methodical approach, as Israel learned
when invading Sinai in 1956. Dayan's
background caused him to favor infantry
while disregarding other combat arms
including tanks, which he saw as expensive,
cumbersome, and prone to breakdown. Armor
therefore had only secondary importance
during Dayan's tenure prior to the Suez Crisis.

Perhaps as a result of his infantry fixation,
or possibly because of Israel's industrial
immaturity, in warfare Dayan preferred the
human dimension to technological prowess.
But in 1955 the IDF's transformation from a
World War II-era force to one with more
modern hardware became urgent when
Egypt obtained Eastern Bloc tanks,

warplanes, and other equipment. France attempted to fill Israel's security void with modern weaponry such as the AMX-13. Speed and a 75 mm gun were important attributes of this tank, but its vulnerability to opposing tank rounds counterbalanced these advantages. By October 1956 Israel had 100 AMX-13s, and a few hundred M4 Sherman (76.2 mm gun) and Super-Sherman (75 mm gun) tanks and M3 half-track troop transports. The Super-Sherman's diesel engine provided resistance to fuel-tank fires.

France also augmented Israel's military capability with state-of-the-art Dassault Mystere IVA and Ouragan single-seat multi-purpose fighters. On the eve of the 1956 Sinai campaign, the Israeli Air Force (IAF) operational inventory included 16 of the former and 22 of the latter. In dogfights, Mysteres outperformed Egypt's new MiGs, while Ouragans excelled in air-to-ground roles such as close air support. Israeli air power doctrine fused these impressive warplanes with Dayan's emphasis on human capabilities. Demanding yet realistic training, a rigorous selection process, and an emphasis on creativity meant that pilot skill almost always surpassed that of Israel's adversaries, especially in aerial combat.

When mobilized for war, Israel could muster roughly 100,000 regular and reserve troops. Of these, slightly fewer than half were available for operations against Egypt. Israel's geography, with Arab adversaries in nearly every direction, required that the remainder of the force stay behind for homeland defense. Since Israel needed to maintain a large military force despite its relatively small population, reservists made up a significant portion of the IDF. By necessity Dayan designated several reserve units for operations in Sinai. Some, such as the 9th Infantry Brigade, excelled despite the demanding conditions in which they fought. Other reserve units, such as the 10th Infantry Brigade, suffered by comparison. When reserve units floundered, it was poor equipment, inadequate training, and Dayan's scattershot mobilization scheme that generally was to blame.

Egypt

Egypt suffered frequent military setbacks prior to the Suez Crisis; in the 1940s humiliating defeats against Britain and Israel contributed to the subsequent demise of King Farouk and his monarchy. Egypt, like all Arab states except Jordan, fought poorly in the 1948–49 war following Israel's creation. A lack of imagination and initiative joined with poor leadership to doom Egypt's 1948 invasion of Israel.

Military leadership improved slightly if at all with the 1952 coup. In both the royal and republican armies, loyalty rather than merit determined promotion; those officers with a powerful patron made rank. Predictably, this arrangement resulted in uneven performance: some officers were competent, but many were not. Field Marshal Abdel Hakim Amer, Egyptian commander-in-chief during the Suez Crisis and subsequent Six-Day War, exemplifies this system's liabilities. Amer owed his position to a close friendship with Nasser rather than to intelligence, charisma, or dedication. Substance abuse clouded his judgement, while self-aggrandizing tendencies eventually compromised his relationship with Nasser. Amer's decisions during the 1956 Sinai campaign reflected his shortcomings. He also neglected the organization and training of Egypt's military forces.

Sophisticated Eastern Bloc hardware failed to mitigate, and in some cases highlighted, these deficiencies, in part because Egyptian troops integrated complex weapons so slowly. More than a year after the 1955 "Czech" arms deal, Egypt was ill-prepared to use its new assault rifles, T-34 and JS3 Stalin tanks, SU100 self-propelled guns, and other advanced weapons despite their impressive capabilities. Since pilot development proved particularly time-consuming, Egypt's air force failed to exploit the performance of its 120 MiG-15 fighters and 50 Ilyushin Il-28 "Beagle" bombers.

Egyptian military forces resembled 18th-century European armies in that rigid separation divided those with commissions from those without. Egypt's middle and upper classes supplied most officers, who typically served a lengthy tenure. Enlisted conscripts, by contrast, came from the lowest social levels in Egypt. Such stratification caused mistrust and contempt, thus weakening Egyptian forces across the board and making offensive operations nearly impossible. Coaxing troops to leave shelter and take the initiative even when they would be exposed to hostile fire requires rapport and effective small-unit leadership, characteristics absent in Egypt's armed forces at the time of the Suez Crisis.

On the defensive, Egypt could fight capably, but counterattacks or other mobile operations rarely succeeded. When troops left their fortifications to fight in the open, they moved slowly and tentatively.

Recognizing this shortcoming, Egypt's leaders emphasized positional warfare. Fixed points, rather than strong leadership, high morale, or innovative doctrine anchored Egyptian defenses in Sinai and elsewhere. This approach collapsed if Egypt's adversaries bypassed these fixed positions and struck from unexpected directions.

In summer 1956, Egypt had about 150,000 soldiers under arms. Nasser allocated roughly a third of these – mostly infantry – to Sinai. The rest, including the bulk of Egyptian armor, he allocated to northern Egypt. The Canal Zone and Mediterranean Sea, primarily along the Nile Delta, had large contingents to repel British or French invasions. In mainland Egypt troops also received training in the use of Egypt's new Eastern Bloc weapons.

Britain, France and Israel contemplate forceful resolution

Preparing for war: plans emerge for Nasser's downfall

Nationalization set in motion events culminating in war three months later. Foremost among these were decisions taken in London, Paris, and Tel Aviv to attack Egypt. Immediately after nationalization, Britain, France, and Israel assessed their military options. Britain and France, called the "Allies" in this context, informally decided upon collaborative efforts to overthrow Nasser; a few weeks later they made these arrangements formal by agreeing to a joint command structure.

Eden's low opinion of Egyptian capabilities manifested itself in his public and private conduct. Riding on a wave of domestic support, he mobilized tens of thousands of reservists, dispatched three aircraft carriers to augment HMS *Eagle* already on station in the Mediterranean, and advocated rapid deployments into Egypt. He suggested that the 16th Independent Parachute Brigade Group capture and occupy the Canal Zone, with additional units to participate as necessary in pursuit of broader British objectives.

Eden's rationale for quick action had many sources. Rapid assaults deprived Egyptian forces of reinforcement opportunities while allowing Eden to capitalize immediately on a "rally around the flag" phenomenon. However, various constraints, including inadequate air- and sea-lift and untrained British paratroops meant unacceptable risk, foreclosing his plan. Eden's chiefs-of-staff, who included Chairman and Chief of the Air Staff Marshal of the Royal Air Force William Dickson, First Sea Lord Earl Mountbatten, and Chief of the Imperial General Staff General Gerald Templer, recognized these shortcomings.

They proposed alternatives built around forces with sufficient training, experience, and equipment. Their creation, the so-called Contingency Plan, relied on sea power and targeted Port Said.

This plan envisaged naval transport of Cyprus- and Malta-based Royal Marines of the 3rd Commando Brigade to the eastern Mediterranean, who would then capture Port Said and seize key airfields and bridges. Additional forces would then be airlifted into the Canal Zone. Entering the theater by sea behind this Royal Marine vanguard would be an occupation force of three British divisions.

Eden's idea and the chiefs' plan, though different, shared key drawbacks. Both emphasized tactics, focusing on the Canal Zone. A strategic vision linking tactical accomplishments to broader success – Nasser's downfall – was, at best, a postscript to both plans. Moreover, neither Eden nor the chiefs described the rationale for military operations; both implicitly assumed that Egyptian nationalization in itself provided sufficient casus belli. World and, in time, domestic opinion contradicted these assumptions.

Perhaps because of these shortcomings, the Contingency Plan evolved through early August, now addressing political considerations to a greater degree while outlining a broader air power role. Additionally, a psychological dimension emerged in the form of strategic air raids that sought to decapitate the Egyptian regime. This facet of the modified Contingency Plan employed bombers to strike Egyptian economic, transportation and communications targets. In ideal circumstances this strategic bombing would make additional military operations, including amphibious assaults, unnecessary.

Furthermore, the modified Contingency Plan added a role for the 16th Independent

Parachute Brigade, somewhat similar to Eden's initial concept. If Nasser withstood strategic bombardment, Britain's military leaders planned to assault the Canal Zone. Paratroops and Royal Marines were to capture Port Said; British reinforcements would then arrive by sea, eliminate any remaining resistance, and occupy most of the Canal.

Though an improvement on the original Contingency Plan, flaws remained. Strategic air warfare against a semi-industrialized state was difficult. Assessing Egyptian infrastructure, political institutions, and morale eluded simple calculations. Port Said posed its own challenges. Operations in this confined area negated British mobility advantages. Also, Port Said lacked support facilities – docks, airfields, and so forth – for a major military endeavor.

British plans evolve: the origins and concept of Musketeer

Thus a few days later, Britain's Task Force commanders – General Hugh Stockwell, Air Marshal Denis Barnett, and Admiral D.F. Durnford-Slater – rejected the Contingency Plan, proposing in its place Operation Musketeer. Musketeer matched Stockwell's military sensibilities, envisaging large, set-piece battles rather than relying on new, relatively unproven techniques such as strategic bombardment and psychological operations.

Although both plans entailed airborne and amphibious assaults, in Musketeer their role paled vis-à-vis the Contingency Plan. Their purpose in Musketeer was simply to secure infantry and armored landing zones. Musketeer air planning stressed tactical considerations such as close air support and interdiction. French General Beaufre advocated an intense two-day air supremacy campaign, after which the RAF and French Air Force could focus on Alexandria, the centerpiece of this new operation.

The abandonment of Port Said marked another major departure from the Contingency Plan. Alexandria, a large port with few geographical constraints, appealed to Allied planners because its facilities lessened the need for landing craft and other amphibious resources. Instead of attempting to break Egypt through air warfare, or depending on scant Anglo-French littoral capabilities, Musketeer sought to annihilate enemy forces in ground combat north of Cairo.

The Contingency Plan and Musketeer shared a common political objective – the overthrow of Nasser – but perceived Egyptian centers of gravity differently. Musketeer saw Nasser's fundamental strength in his fielded forces, while the Contingency Plan assessed political factors as Nasser's key asset. In targeting Egypt's military, Musketeer by necessity required a large ground contingent. Superior experience, training, and doctrine all served as formidable force multipliers for British troops. However, all-out conventional conflict between Nasser's forces and British troops meant that Britain still required tens of thousands of troops in the Egyptian theater to have any chance of victory.

The requirement for enormous ground forces influenced British leaders to pursue more seriously their earlier tentative scheme of coordinating operations with France, which was strongly interested in unseating Nasser. France could supplement British manpower to a point where Musketeer became feasible. French leaders pledged approximately 30,000 troops, including one parachute division and a mechanized division. In tandem with 50,000 British forces, French support gave Britain and France near-parity with Egypt regarding troop levels.

On August 11, Britain and France designated General Keightley as Musketeer's overall commander and Admiral Jobert as his deputy. They established headquarters on Cyprus, a natural choice because of its proximity to Egypt and its three airfields suitable as bases for combat operations. Allied consultations throughout August orchestrated the movement of men, machines, and supplies from Europe to the Mediterranean.

Despite this coincidence of interest, serious challenges remained. France, especially Jobert, preferred Israeli involvement; Eden did not. Collaboration with Israel entailed serious risks to Britain's Middle East positions. Another

point of disagreement concerned Musketeer's preliminaries. French leaders advocated transparent preparations, whereas Eden favored secrecy. His subtlety probably resulted from the influence of the United States.

American pressure for a diplomatic settlement carried more weight in London than Paris. Eisenhower and Dulles distrusted Nasser, particularly his Eastern Bloc dalliances. Thus they favored his removal, the sooner the

President Dwight Eisenhower and Secretary of State John Foster Dulles in Autumn 1956. A re-election campaign occupied much of Eisenhower's time during the Suez Crisis. He and Dulles opposed british and French plans for attacking Egypt. (Topham Picturepoint)

better. But they also thought that the liabilities of military action outweighed its benefits. Eisenhower suggested giving Omega more time. Moreover, he was campaigning for a November re-election, and so hoped to avoid the distraction of a Middle East war.

American influence also contributed to the most vexing aspect of Musketeer, an issue eventually causing its demise: the challenge of reconciling diplomatic timelines with a complex military schedule. Extensive lead times within Musketeer meant a significant delay between Britain and France deciding to invade Egypt and actually invading. Beaufre, who helped plan Musketeer, initially estimated this delay at three weeks. This interval later shrank by a week, but remained large enough to cause anxiety among British and French leaders.

Eden in particular fretted about schedules. He hoped to explore – nominally at least – every peaceful alternative, yet an armada steaming across the Mediterranean during diplomatic talks weakened his commitment to bona fide negotiations. However, Eden lacked the luxury of time, since Mediterranean weather typically deteriorated in late autumn, precluding most amphibious and naval operations. These countervailing forces – diplomatic delays versus meteorological urgency – trapped Eden in a temporal nutcracker.

Dulles and Eden conversing. (Topham Picturepoint)

Revise replaces Musketeer

Interestingly, a solution appeared from across the English Channel. In late August, Barjot proposed abandoning Alexandria and restoring Port Said as the invasion site. Although this shift reduced the scope of military operations, thereby diminishing the delay between deciding to invade and actually invading, British leaders and even Barjot's subordinate, Beaufre, at first disdained his idea. Barjot's rationale for proposing this radical change remains obscure. Certainly one factor was his interest in establishing a role for Israel, with whom military connections blossomed throughout 1956. Conflict centered at Port Said rather than Alexandria made Israeli involvement much more feasible. Also, compared with other British and French leaders, Barjot showed less interest in toppling Nasser than in capturing limited objectives and using these as diplomatic bargaining chips.

This notion rankled Beaufre, who feared that an ambiguous blend of politics and warfare might undercut the Egyptian campaign. For Beaufre, nagging questions attended Barjot's proposal. When would hostilities cease? How long could forces be sustained in the Canal Zone? What if post-combat diplomacy failed to produce the desired outcome? Furthermore, unlike most others involved in strategic planning, Beaufre understood that Britain and France needed the Suez Canal more than Egypt did, meaning that their negotiating position vis-à-vis Egypt suffered if Canal traffic ceased for any reason. Invading Port Said carried the significant risk of interrupting Canal transit. For Beaufre, therefore, Barjot's plan seemed counterproductive.

Stockwell shared Beaufre's reservations about a Canal Zone campaign, but Keightley soon warmed to the idea. In early September he proposed Operation Revise, fusing the earlier Contingency Plan with Barjot's idea for invading Port Said. Although Musketeer and Revise shared a common objective – Nasser's downfall – the methods for attaining this goal in Revise radically departed from Musketeer. Strategic bombing replaced amphibious assaults on Alexandria and a subsequent overland campaign to Cairo as the British and French instrument to destroy Nasser. Keightley outlined Revise thus:

Phase I: Britain and France to gain air superiority

Phase II: A 10-day "aero-psychological" campaign to overthrow Nasser, combining strikes at transportation, communication, and economic centers with an assault on Egyptian morale

Phase III: After Phase II toppled Nasser, Anglo-French airborne and amphibious forces to occupy the Canal Zone

The enormous political dimension of the Suez Crisis became evident on September 8, when British and French leaders approved Revise. Stockwell and Beaufre despised this open-ended plan, but Eden and others saw Revise as superior to Musketeer. Civilian casualties would be fewer and the campaign smaller, cheaper, and more flexible, giving political leaders more options in their ongoing diplomacy and military preparations. Another factor favoring Revise was the fear of intelligence leaks regarding Musketeer preparations. These considerations tipped the balance in favor of Revise over the objections of many military commanders.

After abandoning Musketeer, Britain and France immediately established Revise schedules. Initial timetables outlined an October 1 D-Day, but, just as had been the case with Musketeer, political necessity forced several slips of the Revise D-Day. Several bureaucratic annoyances remained, such as UN Security Council involvement. Eden also lacked a defensible pretext for invading Egypt. By late September, D-Day was on indefinite hold. Britain and France began preparing the Winter Plan, a scheme for maintaining long-term Revise readiness.

Israel builds Kadesh

Although Israel remained outside Revise, provisions for invading Egypt predated the Suez Crisis by several months. Preparations began in 1955 when a small Israeli reconnaissance patrol, Operation Yarkon, scouted the route to Sharm el-Sheikh, assessing eastern Sinai and its suitability for mechanized movement. Planning intensified after Nasser's September arms deal and his decision to tighten the Tiran Straits blockade. These developments prompted many Israelis to advocate pre-emptive attacks against Egypt. In December 1955, Dayan recommended capturing the Tiran Straits. His government rejected these suggestions, which languished through mid-1956 despite frequent boundary clashes.

After the Suez Crisis erupted, Nasser responded to Musketeer preparations by shifting forces from Sinai to the Delta and Suez Canal Zone. This redeployment presented a golden opportunity, so Israel resurrected earlier plans for increasing its security vis-à-vis Egypt. In this updated operation, Kadesh, Dayan carefully articulated Israeli doctrine, stressing air superiority, mobility and encirclement rather than attrition. At the outset of the campaign, Israeli warplanes were to destroy Egypt's air force on the ground, then shift to close air support missions.

Once ground combat began, Dayan predicted that waging "one continuous battle" would result in fluid situations, propelling Israel to victory. On the battlefield, Israeli forces had an edge over their Egyptian adversaries owing to their superior initiative and training. Dayan identified "dominant positions of tactical importance" as key centers of gravity, providing Kadesh an over-arching theme – the conquest of Sinai – and four narrower objectives. The most important of these related to the Aqaba Gulf blockade, which Egypt based at Sharm el-Sheikh and Ras Nasrani. To open the Tiran Straits, Dayan planned to capture these localities. Dayan also targeted al-Arish and Abu Uwayulah, bases in northern and central Sinai which

might be used for potential attacks on Israel. Finally, Israel sought to destroy through conquest Gaza's *fedayeen* training and support areas.

Dayan's fascination with encirclement prompted an "outside-in" approach to accomplishing campaign goals. He planned to capture distant objectives first, and then shift to closer targets. Thus Dayan designated the 202nd Paratroop Brigade, under the command of Colonel Ariel Sharon, to initiate Kadesh by parachuting into northwestern Sinai and cutting Egyptian supply lines, facilitating attacks on al-Arish and Abu Uwayulah. Dayan also planned a simultaneous paratroop attack near the Aqaba Gulf, targeting Sharm el-Sheikh and Ras Nasrani. Finally, Israel would hit Gaza, the objective closest to Israeli territory.

Dayan wrestled with Kadesh mobilization schedules, the timing of which posed several challenges. Mobilizing at an early stage simplified Israel's preparations, but also telegraphed its intentions to Israel's adversaries. Therefore Dayan opted for delay, deciding to mobilize the IDF only a few days before Kadesh began.

Collusion at Sevres

By mid-October, Dayan's plan for the conquest of Sinai had matured. Soon, however, developments elsewhere forced Dayan to reconsider Kadesh. After resisting for two months French efforts to include Israel in their anti-Nasser coalition, Eden changed course, probably out of desperation. He required a plausible excuse for launching Revise; covertly teaming up with Israel was perhaps his only short-term option. Winter's approach and deteriorating equipment shrank the window of opportunity for military operations. Waiting for spring jeopardized the possibility of any action against Nasser.

After deciding to collude with Israel, Eden established specific arrangements through late-October tripartite meetings in Sevres, France. Here Britain, France, and Israel outlined responsibilities for their forthcoming military campaign. Britain and France asked Israel to provide a reason for attacking Egypt commensurate with Revise. Israel, fearing retaliatory raids by Ilyushin Il-28 "Beagle" bombers, in turn requested Britain and France to destroy these jets. British and French representatives agreed, in part because Revise Phase I already outlined the destruction of Egypt's air force, including all bombers. The three nations agreed to this sequence, also known as the Sevres Protocol:

October 29: Israel attacks Egypt near the Suez Canal

October 30: Britain and France demand Israel and Egypt withdraw from the Canal

October 31: Upon the ultimatum's morning expiry, Britain and France initiate Revise Phase I

To accommodate these altered circumstances, Dayan revised Kadesh. He established a catalyst to precipitate British and French involvement by threatening the Canal. Although the earliest, pre-Sevres iteration of Kadesh unintentionally filled this mandate through attacks in northwestern Sinai, Dayan shifted to west-central Sinai at Mitla Pass. He probably hoped to convey an impression to Egypt that Israeli action was a raid rather than a full-blown invasion.

Dayan also modified schedules. Pre-Sevres, Kadesh plunged straightaway into Egypt with full weight and force. After Sevres, immediate attacks no longer matched Israel's interests. Rather, disguising intent became paramount. Thus Dayan attempted to portray Israeli mobilization as a preparation for attacking Jordan. Israeli forces, especially armored formations but including even the 202nd Paratroop Brigade, were to limit Sinai operations until Revise Phase I. In addition to

Mitla, only Sinai's eastern gateways – Nizzana, al-Qusaymah, al-Kuntillah, and Ras an-Naqb – were subject to early attack. These constraints allowed Israel to abandon Sinai if France and Britain reneged on their commitments.

Finally, Dayan changed the role of the IAF, which was no longer responsible for securing air superiority now that Britain and France were partners of Israel. The air force missions shifted from strategic to operational and tactical: air cover, close air support and interdiction in Sinai. As aerial operations west of Sinai might provoke Egypt to bomb Israeli cities, Dayan prohibited them unless Ilyushin jets attacked Israel.

Dayan then assembled four Kadesh combat groups, deploying them along geographical lines. Responsibility for the northern axis – a corridor whose hub was al-Arish, adjacent to the Mediterranean and linking Rafah with al-Qantarah – and Gaza rested with the three brigades (two infantry and one armored) of Brigadier General Haim Lascov's division-sized Group 77. Colonel Yehudah Wallach's Group 38, also division-sized, operated along the central axis, stretching across Sinai from Ketziot to al-Ismailiyah. This force, the strongest of those in Sinai, had four brigades, two infantry and two armored.

Since only the 2nd Egyptian Motorized Border Battalion defended the southern axis, which stretched from frontier outposts near the 1949 armistice line through Mitla Pass to the city of Suez roughly 322 km (200 miles) west, Dayan expected minimal Egyptian resistance. He also understood its purely political function, so allocated it a single brigade, the 202nd Paratroop. His only goal was to threaten the Canal at minimum risk to Israeli forces. Despite the significance of Sinai's Aqaba axis, Egypt deployed few forces here. Therefore Dayan assigned responsibility for this area to a reserve infantry brigade.

Crisis becomes war

War in Sinai

Kadesh in motion: 202nd Paratroop Brigade v. southern axis

Israeli mobilization began on October 24 as the Sevres talks concluded. Dayan at first authorized a partial mobilization, which proceeded in an almost casual fashion. Mailed notices alerted reservists to report for duty at various staging areas, while requisitions went out for support vehicles. When this experiment failed, Dayan

Lieutenant Colonel Rafael Eytan commanded 1st Battalion, 202nd Paratroop Brigade, which parachuted into west-central Sinai at Parker's Memorial on 29 October 1956. Eytan and his men held off Egyptian attacks until the remainder of the brigade arrived some 30 hours later. (Topham Picturepoint)

expedited military preparation, ordering all-out mobilization despite the risk of alerting Egypt. Surprisingly, these drastic measures succeeded in attaining a high level of readiness without sacrificing secrecy. By October 29 most Kadesh units had reached their Negev staging areas.

Kadesh commenced at 03:00 pm that day when Israeli Mustangs attacked Egypt's Sinai communications network. An hour later the 202nd Paratroop Brigade entered Egypt with the politically significant but militarily marginal assignment of "raiding" Sinai, thereby triggering the Sevres Protocol. Sharon's goal was in western Sinai, but his brigade assembled at Ein-Hussub near Jordan to preserve secrecy.

This unusual deployment fooled Nasser, but also imposed significant hardships on Sharon. Before invading Egypt, the 202nd Paratroop Brigade traveled southern Israel's primitive roads and trails. The brigade would then face many miles of unpaved Sinai tracks. Sharon's planning assumed access to hundreds of front-wheel drive French trucks, which unlike rear-wheel drive trucks could negotiate difficult terrain. Shortly before H-Hour, Sharon learned that his brigade had but a fraction of its original vehicle allotment. Undeterred, three battalions of the 202nd Paratroop Brigade entered Egypt in mid-afternoon, 29 October. About half Sharon's contingent of 13 AMX-13 tanks survived the journey to Sinai. As these forces slogged westwards, the 1st (sometimes designated the 890th) Battalion, 202nd Paratroop Brigade, passed overhead aboard four four-ship cells of Douglas DC-3 Dakotas with Gloucester Meteor escort, their objective Mitla Pass.

Rather than a traditional "pass" – a low point adjoining higher features – Mitla is multiple defiles through the Jebel

Heitan/Jebel Giddi massif. From east to west, these gaps are Heitan Defile, the "Saucer," and Mitla Defile. The 1st Battalion initially planned to jump at Mitla Defile, the area's most defensible terrain. However, aerial reconnaissance indicated Egyptians in the vicinity, and Israeli anxiety about dropping paratroopers directly onto an enemy strongpoint compelled changes. The 1st Battalion would drop near a crossroads east of Jebel Heitan at Parker's Memorial and march to Heitan Defile.

As Israeli DC-3s approached the Memorial, nearly 400 paratroops leapt into twilit Sinai skies. A quick landscape survey while under canopy indicated that rather than jumping at the Memorial, they had actually parachuted three miles from their intended drop zone, and five miles from their ultimate destination, Heitan Defile. Subsequent investigation revealed that a navigation error caused the mistake, which had deadly consequences for Israeli forces.

Upon landing, the 1st Battalion marched through darkness for two hours. When they encountered small slopes, battalion commander and future IDF chief-of-staff Rafael Eytan, confused by the poor visibility, halted a mile east of Jebel Heitan. His battalion then entrenched. Here, under orders to avoid combat, Eytan coordinated French aerial delivery of mortars, anti-tank weapons, recoilless guns, and jeeps. These came via a Nord Aviation NordAtlas 2501 drop on the evening of 29 October. The paratroops, bivouacked within minefields and barbed wire and repulsing several Egyptian probes, awaited Sharon, who had assured Dayan he could reach Mitla in 24 hours.

He was overly optimistic. Poor logistics caused serious challenges. The 202nd Paratroop Brigade sputtered westwards as more and more vehicles succumbed to the relentless desert. Egyptian fortifications en route also held up their progress. At dusk on D-Day, the brigade attacked al-Kuntillah, a plateau outpost 19 km(12 miles) from Israel. Al-Kuntillah's defenders followed their orders, retreating into darkness without resisting Israel's attack. Sharon pushed onwards, hoping to keep to his schedule. He ordered all functional vehicles to attack Themed, 30 miles southwest. Slower units could catch up when possible. Sharon's obsession with speed during darkness was due to two factors. Egyptian military pilots, preferring visual flight rules to instrument navigation, posed little danger at night. Moreover, Sharon hoped to reach the 1st Battalion before Egypt reinforced Mitla Pass.

Early Israeli action on the Central and Aqaba axes

While the 202nd Paratroop Brigade approached Themed, along the Aqaba Gulf the 9th Infantry Brigade attacked Ras an-Naqb. This isolated outpost along a confluence of desert paths a dozen miles west of Eilat had twofold Kadesh significance. One path veering northwest from Ras an-Naqb screened Sharon's flank. Another path followed the Aqaba Gulf towards Ras Nasrani and Sharm el-Sheikh. These locales, the ultimate objective for the 9th Infantry Brigade, made Ras an-Naqb an ideal staging area to advance in their direction. To capture this outpost, the 9th Infantry Brigade employed typical Israeli tactics, striking from unexpected directions at night. Patrols used natural features to facilitate movement and bypassed Egyptian positions by traversing rough terrain. By midnight on October 30, Israel had seized Ras an-Naqb while sustaining no casualties.

While the 9th Infantry Brigade fought near Eilat, further north Israel's 4th Infantry Brigade, under the command of Colonel Josef Harpaz, attempted to gain lost time. Kadesh directed Harpaz to storm al-Qusaymah, a border outpost near a key intersection, one hour before midnight. Multiple paths converged there. Control of one protected the 202nd Paratroop Brigade's northern flank along the southern axis. Another artery, this one a paved road, led northwest to the Abu Uwayulah Hedgehog, home to Egyptian fortifications and key intersections in northern Sinai. The 4th Infantry Brigade's primary obstacle was terrain. Southern commander General Asaf

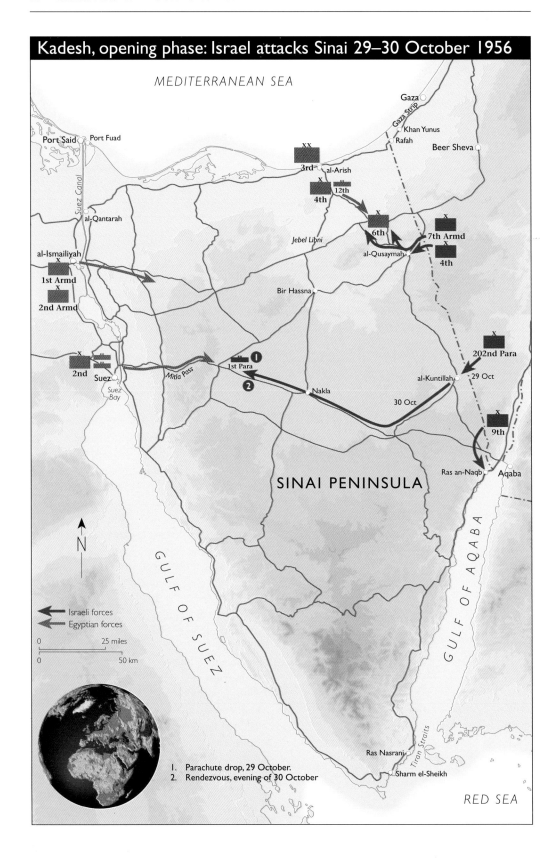

Kadesh, opening phase: Israel attacks Sinai 29–30 October 1956

MEDITERRANEAN SEA

Gaza

Gaza Strip

Port Said   Port Fuad

Khan Yunus

Rafah

Beer Sheva

XX

3rd   al-Arish

X

12th

4th

X

6th

X

7th Armd

Jebel Libni

X

al-Qusaymah   4th

al-Qantarah

al-Ismailiyah

X

1st Armd

X

2nd Armd

Bir Hassna

X

202nd Para

X

2nd   Suez

Mitla Pass   1st Para ①

②

Suez
Bay

Nakla   al-Kuntillah   29 Oct

30 Oct

X

9th

Ras an-Naqb   Aqaba

SINAI PENINSULA

N

GULF OF SUEZ

GULF OF AQABA

→ Israeli forces
→ Egyptian forces

0   25 miles
0   50 km

Ras Nasrani

Tiran Straits

1. Parachute drop, 29 October.
2. Rendezvous, evening of 30 October.

Sharm el-Sheikh

RED SEA

Simhoni ordered Harpaz's brigade to seize al-Qusaymah by dawn on 30 October. Even before leaving Israel, Harpaz knew the difficulty this timetable presented. Only front-wheel drive trucks – a fraction of his fleet – could negotiate sand. With most vehicles disabled, the 4th Infantry Brigade's troops struggled to keep pace.

Harpaz flanked al-Qusaymah, his pincers developing from northeast and southeast, then converging on Jebel al-Sabha, key terrain east of al-Qusaymah. The northern arm used a road, but the southern column bushwhacked in darkness through punishing terrain. Egyptian forces at al-Qusaymah numbered two battalions and two companies armed with machine guns, mortars, and half-tracks. Most occupied Jebel al-Sabha. Although the southern Israeli pincer arrived several hours late, Harpaz's attack proceeded according to plan.

At 03:00 am, 30 October, the 4th Infantry Brigade hit Jebel al-Sabha's dual hills, and Egyptian formations soon collapsed. Mop-up operations lasted until sunrise; the brigade then entered a deserted al-Qusaymah, on schedule and basically intact, where Israeli tanks joined them. On a pretext that the 4th Infantry Brigade was behind schedule, Simhoni released the 7th Armored Brigade from dormancy at Nahal Ruth, violating standing orders. Simhoni was to commit no armor until 31 October; doing so revealed the breadth of Israeli operations, and might trigger all-out war.

202nd Paratroop Brigade and the battle of Jebel Heitan

While Simhoni violated Dayan's orders, the 202nd Paratroop Brigade advanced, at midnight reaching Themed. Although this outpost functioned primarily as a police and customs detachment, its larger garrison (a Sudanese company), better armaments, and stronger defenses vis-à-vis al-Kuntillah posed a more difficult challenge. Minefields and terrain channeled attacks towards its defenders. Sharon struck at dawn despite

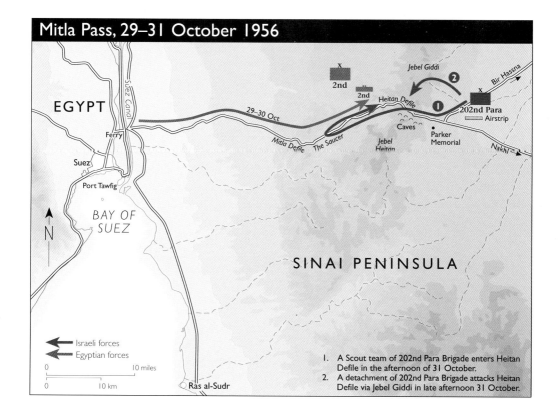

Mitla Pass, 29–31 October 1956

EGYPT

SINAI PENINSULA

Suez Canal

Ferry

Suez

Port Tawfig

BAY OF SUEZ

N

Ras al-Sudr

29–30 Oct

Mitla Defile   The Saucer

Jebel Heitan

Caves

Parker Memorial

Jebel Heitan

Heitan Defile

2nd

2nd

Jebel Giddi

Bir Hassna

202nd Para
Airstrip

Nakhl

→ Israeli forces
→ Egyptian forces

0   10 miles
0   10 km

1. A Scout team of 202nd Para Brigade enters Heitan Defile in the afternoon of 31 October.
2. A detachment of 202nd Para Brigade attacks Heitan Defile via Jebel Giddi in late afternoon 31 October.

limited artillery. A fickle ally, the sun, assisted him. Assaulting at dawn blinded Egyptian eyes, obscuring Sharon's movements until his forces closed to short range. Israeli armor then stormed Themed Gap, overwhelming Sudanese defenders atop a rock wall. Now 97 km (60 miles) and a final strongpoint, Nakla, separated Sharon from the 1st Battalion. With victory within reach, he advanced while arranging medical evacuation. If all went well, the 202nd Paratroop Brigade might soon reunite near Mitla.

One setback in an otherwise successful campaign soon arose. Having earlier declined to attack the 1st Battalion, Egyptian Vampires and MiG-15s appeared along the central axis, striking both detachments of the 202nd Paratroop Brigade. Despite some losses to these raids, the 202nd Paratroop Brigade reached Nakla the afternoon of 30 October. Israeli artillery barrages quickly broke Egyptian morale, allowing Sharon and his vanguard to rendezvous with Eytan that night after a 30-hour journey.

Before Sharon arrived at Mitla, other faraway developments escalated Israeli–Egyptian hostilities. In Parliament on 30 October, Eden directed Egypt and Israel to "withdraw military forces ... 16 km (10 miles) from the Canal." Failure to do so would mean "intervention ... to secure compliance," Eden warned. His ultimatum, which British diplomats handed to their Egyptian and Israeli counterparts, fulfilled Britain's initial Sevres obligations, and started the Revise countdown.

As Britain, France, and Israel expected, Nasser – who perceived Eden's speech as a ruse – objected, instead reinforcing Sinai and seeking to destroy Eytan's battalion, which on 30 October endured a long day. Two battalions of the 2nd Egyptian Infantry Brigade crossed into Sinai the previous night, marching east to Jebel Heitan despite numerous IAF attacks once the sun rose. Other Egyptian patrols occupied Parker's Memorial, depriving Eytan of defensible terrain and forcing him to the low ground east of Heitan Defile. From above came small arms and machine gun fire.

Upon consolidating his brigade, Sharon pondered his next move. Attacking Mitla Pass seemed tactically attractive, but standing orders prohibited any such action. Also, darkness and fog obscured visibility; these factors, in tandem with troop fatigue, restricted his short-term choices. Dawn found Sharon impatiently surveying his surroundings. His unease had several sources. First, he and his paratroops embraced offensive as opposed to defensive operations (see "Portrait of a soldier"). Reports of the 1st and 2nd Egyptian Armored Brigades of the 4th Egyptian Armored Division a few dozen miles north of Mitla Pass heightened Sharon's disquiet. On open ground T-34s and SU100 self-propelled guns could annihilate the 202nd Paratroop Brigade's half-tracks and AMX-13s. Unaware that Israeli armor screened him from these forces, and IAF attacks left his enemy incapable of offensive operations, Sharon wanted better terrain. Recent aerial reconnaissance indicating no enemy movement in Heitan Defile provided an additional incentive for capturing higher ground. Aside from these considerations, however, Sharon misunderstood Dayan's broader framework, which never envisaged Sharon striking west towards the Canal. A common criticism of Sharon is that he suffers from strategic myopia, and this condition apparently prevailed on 31 October. His decision to advance into Heitan Defile caused needless Israeli casualties and slowed the 202nd Paratroop Brigade's subsequent advance towards Sharm el-Sheikh.

Sharon, favoring tactics over strategy, consulted Dayan early on 31 October, hoping to reverse the ban on seizing Mitla. Rebuffed, he proposed scouting Heitan Defile. Dayan approved, cautioning Sharon to "avoid ... serious combat." Thus Sharon assembled an assault force – much larger than a mere scout team – under the command of future Israeli chief-of-staff Major Mordecai Gur. This contingent – two companies, a mortar battery, three half-tracks and a few AMX-13s – entered Heitan Defile on the afternoon of 31 October. Gur soon learned that morning intelligence reports, which neither he nor Sharon had independently verified, were incorrect. Egyptian forces now occupied Heitan Defile's textured walls, using caves and ledges to direct mortar, anti-tank, and machine gun fire against Gur's team. Sharon, in his haste to storm the heights, disregarded all caution, accepted favorable intelligence as gospel, and sent his men into the Heitan deathtrap.

Dayan later criticized Sharon for his conduct at Jebel Heitan. Perhaps surprisingly, Dayan publicly faulted Sharon primarily for tactics rather than disobedience. Dayan thought that encircling Jebel Heitan and Jebel Giddi along their gentler southern and northern slopes offered the best prospect for success. Attacking in column into a well-defended gorge provided excellent opportunities for enemy ambush – precisely what happened as Gur entered the Heitan Defile. As Gur's commandos came under fire they sought cover or at least easier terrain at the "Saucer." However, an Egyptian wreck blocked their path; the commandos moved it, but lost their last operational half-track. At the "Saucer" small groups found relief from Egyptian crossfire, but Gur's force was now split and rock walls interfered with radio communication, thus preventing a rendezvous.

Seven hours of chaos followed. AMX-13s repeatedly fired their 75 mm shells against an invisible enemy; Egyptian half-tracks hidden among the canyon's bends and curves raked Gur's men with machine gun fire. Vampires and MiGs pounded Israelis in the "Saucer" and further east. Fortunately for Gur, Israeli aircraft above western Sinai prevented Egyptian warplanes from multiple attacks. Hoping to extricate Gur, Sharon dispatched to Jebel Giddi another force, which subsequently descended the canyon while Gur's force scaled cliffs on either side of the defile, trapping Egyptians in the north wall. Darkness turned the battle into a rout. Israeli commandos, now much less exposed than during daylight, thrived in these conditions whereas Egyptians struggled. Soon the 202nd Paratroop Brigade cleared every cave, ending the engagement. Israel inflicted heavy casualties, killing over 200 Egyptians, but sustaining 38 deaths as well.

Hunting a Hedgehog: Israel storms Abu Uwayulah

Hedgehog dispositions and topography

Simhoni's premature armor commitment on 30 October was due to the importance of the central axis. Abu Uwayulah village, 32 km (20 miles) west of Nizzana, naturally caught his interest. This settlement amidst several paved roads was Sinai's most important transportation hub. As Kennett Love observes, nearby roads make "perfect [flanking] avenues" regarding Sinai's northern and southern axes. Israeli control of these arteries exposed Egyptian forces to encirclement.

East of Abu Uwayulah, itself indefensible, ridges – Ruafa, Umm Shihan, and Umm Qataf – comprise a zone known as the Hedgehog. During the first day of a three-day battle here, Colonel Sami Yassa commanded roughly 3000 Egyptians. Two battalions, the 17th and 18th of the 6th Infantry Brigade, 3rd Infantry Division, constituted his primary strength. Nearby were three other companies, an artillery regiment, and two anti-tank batteries. Earlier that decade Egypt had augmented its Hedgehog positions; European advisors developed bunkers, trenches, and artillery enabling mutual defenses and fire support.

Favorable geography, meanwhile, limited attack options. North lay an expanse of dunes; to the south rose the Jebel Halal, Jebel Dalfa, and Jebel Wugeir promontories. Through a valley in this massif came a path from al-Qusaymah, the settlement against which Simhoni committed the 7th Armored Brigade on 30 October. Hills immediately adjacent to the al-Qusaymah track facilitated defensive positions there. Thus, ground assaults could hit only two sides of the Hedgehog – Umm Qataf's east flank and Ruafa's west flank – and only the former seemed truly susceptible to immediate overland attack. Yassa, concerned that Israel might attack his west flank with airborne troops, split available forces, positioning one battalion and anti-tank battery on his east flank and another of each to the west. South

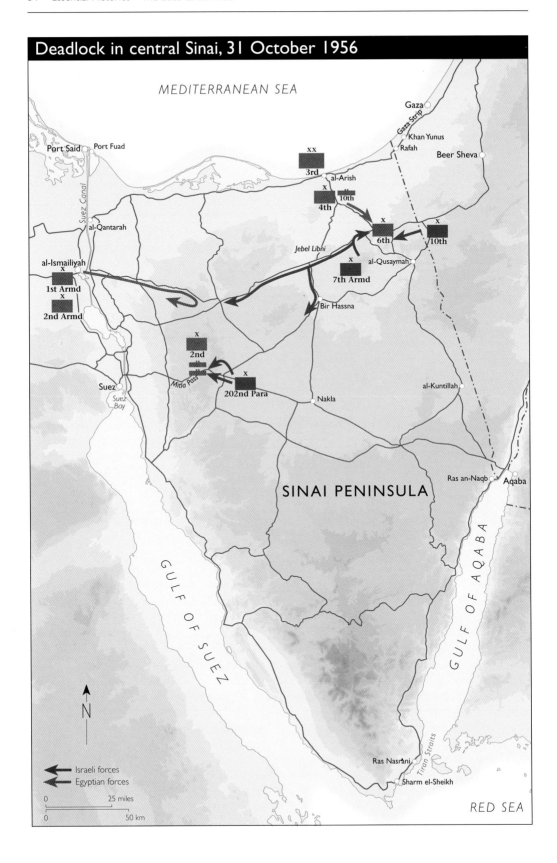

Deadlock in central Sinai, 31 October 1956

MEDITERRANEAN SEA

Gaza

Port Said   Port Fuad

Gaza Strip

Khan Yunus

Rafah

Beer Sheva

xx

3rd

al-Arish

x

4th

x

10th

Suez Canal

al-Qantarah

x

6th

x

10th

al-Ismailiyah

x

1st Armd

x

2nd Armd

Jebel Libni

x

7th Armd

al-Qusaymah

Bir Hassna

x

2nd

Suez

Suez
Bay

Mitla Pass

x

202nd Para

Nakla

al-Kuntillah

SINAI PENINSULA

Ras an-Naqb   Aqaba

GULF OF SUEZ

GULF OF AQABA

Tiran Straits

Ras Nasrani

Sharm el-Sheikh

RED SEA

N

Israeli forces
Egyptian forces

0   25 miles

0   50 km

of Umm Shihan, Jebel Dalfa overlooked each ridge, so Yassa placed his artillery regiment there. He also dispersed infantry patrols along his periphery.

Numerical disadvantages, in which Simhoni outnumbered Yassa four to one at the Hedgehog, constituted a fatal liability, however. The challenge to the Egyptians of holding their positions against this manpower became apparent on 30 October, after al-Qusaymah fell at dawn to the 4th Infantry Brigade. Two Israeli pincers – infantry from the east and armor from the south – converged on Umm Qataf in advance of the Kadesh master schedule. Dayan planned to move against the Hedgehog at least one day later, after Revise Phase I. However, Simhoni's rash decision to reinforce the 4th Infantry Brigade at al-Qusaymah with the 7th Armored Brigade compromised this timetable. Having committed his tanks to battle, Simhoni assigned Major Izhak Ben-Ari to probe the Hedgehog while cautioning him to avoid daytime combat.

Israel probes the Hedgehog: 30 October

However, Ben-Ari's reconnaissance soon became an all-out attack against Umm Qataf. Joining Yassa's 18th Infantry Battalion in defending this position was much of the 17th Infantry Battalion, having recently traveled five miles from Ruafa. Yassa himself fought, but a trauma brought on by his preparations for an Egyptian counterattack forced his medical evacuation. Egyptian forces nonetheless easily prevailed; artillery and anti-tank fire claimed several tanks, shattering Ben-Ari's attack.

Others in the 7th Armored Brigade had more success that day. South of Abu Uwayulah, Ben-Ari's motorized patrol scouting Jebel Halal, a plateau anchoring the Hedgehog's edge, located a gap, al-Dayyiqa, cleaving the high ground. By capturing this pass Israel could capitalize on a key opportunity. Freed from the confines of attacking on a single viable axis (the east), Israeli forces could assail the western front as

well. To some extent Yassa understood al-Dayyiqa's significance but he inadequately defended this key position. Manpower constraints forced him to guard the cleft with one platoon. Having neither armor nor artillery, this unit attempted to destroy, not defend, the pass, but its efforts failed. As a 7th Armored Brigade reconnaissance team approached, Egyptian sentries blew a bridge just south of al-Dayyiqa, detonated charges strewn among its walls, and fled.

Their efforts to obliterate the pass made Israeli transit difficult, but not impossible. After struggling amid craters and fallen boulders, the scout team emerged near Abu Uwayulah. Apparently, in planning al-Dayyiqa's defense, Yassa assumed he could summon air power to blast hostile forces threading through the narrow defile. Such assistance failed to appear that day, although explanations remain elusive. Perhaps the Egyptian air force ignored Yassa's call for air strikes; maybe his incapacitation prevented him from requesting support at all.

Clearly, however, the 7th Armored Brigade's success at al-Dayyiqa weakened the Hedgehog. Israel could now hit both flanks, placing Yassa's successor, Colonel Saadedden Mutawally, in a dilemma. Should he continue massing in the eastern Hedgehog? Converging Israeli pincers persuaded Mutawally to do so. He thought that the greatest danger to his position would develop at Umm Qataf. In addition to the 7th Armored Brigade's afternoon onslaught against the Hedgehog, the 10th Infantry Brigade, Colonel Shmuel Gudir commanding, also attacked. Gudir's lead elements stormed and captured Auja Masri and Tarat Um Basis, outposts east of Umm Qataf.

Mutawally's conclusion, however, showed his relative ignorance of the Hedgehog. Unaccustomed to his new post, he neglected a grave threat: the 7th Armored Brigade's western flanking maneuver. This pincer developed slowly. For 12 hours Major Ben-Ari and Israeli scouts, miles from friendly forces, guarded al-Dayyiqa while Lieutenant Colonel Avraham Adan and his battalion traversed the pass in darkness with their armor. En route Adan abandoned wheeled vehicles as these could not negotiate rocky obstacles. Accompanying Adan on this treacherous slog was Colonel Ben-Ari, who earlier on 30 October split his unit three ways. One group rolled west, attempting to screen the 202nd Paratroop Brigade from the 1st and 2nd Armored Brigades assembling in western Sinai. Meanwhile, Adan's formation led the reinforcement effort through al-Dayyiqa; another armored battalion followed. Their primary task was storming Ruafa, the Hedgehog's west flank.

Israeli attacks at the Hedgehog

Adan and roughly 80 tracked vehicles left al-Dayyiqa at first light, 31 October, assembled on the al-Ismailiyah–Ruafa road, and drove three miles east. Here at the Abu Uwayulah crossroads, Egyptian positions blocked the route to Ruafa. Open terrain made defending this junction difficult, but its proximity to high ground allowed Mutawally to employ

Hedgehog firepower against attacking Israeli forces. As an Egyptian company in Abu Uwayulah shot rockets and machine gun rounds, artillery and anti-tank barrages from Jebel Dalfa destroyed a few tanks. After an hour-long melee, though, Israeli armor flanked and routed their enemy.

Ben-Ari deployed one 7th Armored Brigade battalion to the west once it traversed al-Dayyiqa, placing with Adan the sole responsibility for striking Ruafa. Storming well-defended positions atop commanding heights was challenging, and became more difficult shortly before noon when the 10th Infantry Battalion, 3rd Egyptian Infantry Division, attempted to reinforce the 12th Infantry Battalion at Ruafa. From his al-Arish headquarters, division commander Brigadier General Anwar al-Qadi belatedly dispatched

Occupation duty: British Cpl John Grimwood digs in along the Suez Canal (to his left) at al-Cap Station on the road to al-Ismailiyah, 12 November 1956. (TRH Pictures)

this unit to the Hedgehog. His decision to send the 10th Infantry Battalion south on the morning of 31 October, rather than deploying it immediately to Abu Uwayulah upon learning of Israeli success at al-Dayyiqa as he had done with the 12th Infantry Battalion, was a mistake. Daytime movement left the 10th Infantry Battalion vulnerable to ferocious Israeli air strikes, which demolished several Shermans and inflicted heavy casualties.

Also, advance Israeli units had already severed connections to Ruafa once these Egyptian reinforcements arrived. If the 10th Infantry Battalion hoped to enter the Hedgehog and augment the 12th Infantry Battalion, it first had to engage an Israeli armored battalion. Better options for al-Qadi included keeping the 10th Infantry Battalion near al-Arish, where reinforcement of Rafah was still possible, or, if long-range movement became unavoidable, doing so at night.

As these developments proceeded near Abu Uwayulah, 16 km (10 miles) east the 10th Infantry Brigade struck the Hedgehog, encountering heavy Egyptian fire. Dayan, ascribing this failure to inadequate preparation, poor leadership, and sluggish

Tankers of Israeli's 7th Armoured Brigade reload their Sherman tanks in central Sinai. The wheeled vehicle's entrapment along the right side of this picture depicts the difficulty of traveling in arduous Sinai terrain. (Topham Picturepoint)

battlefield performance, granted the 10th Infantry Brigade a short respite before resuming the assault. Dayan's third criticism at least is misplaced. Demanding that infantry with a small armored contingent (half-tracks at that) overrun prepared positions atop strong terrain in daylight with only a slight numerical advantage (just less than 2:1) is to ask the impossible. Even the 7th Armored Brigade, with its greater firepower, failed under similar circumstances.

While the 10th Infantry Brigade convalesced, the 7th Armored Brigade drove west towards the 1st and 2nd Egyptian Armored Brigade's tanks and self-propelled artillery. By noon, 31 October, Israel had seized crucial junctions at Jebel Libni and Bir Hassna; the 7th Armored Brigade then advanced to Bir Hama, just east of suspected Egyptian positions. Meanwhile the IAF devastated enemy armor concentrations but also attacked friendly forces. Ouragans and

Abu Aoueigila, 30 October–1 November 1956

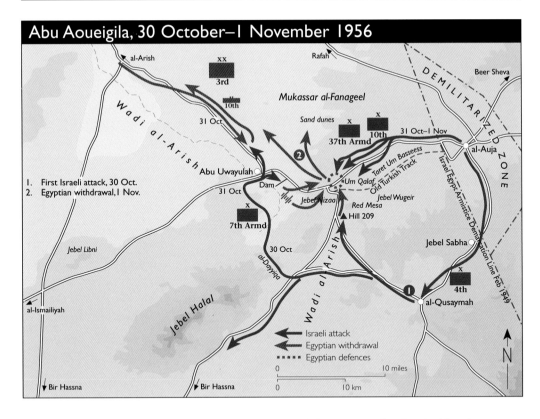

1. First Israeli attack, 30 Oct.
2. Egyptian withdrawal, 1 Nov.

Israeli attack
Egyptian withdrawal
Egyptian defences

0 _____ 10 miles
0 _____ 10 km

Mysteres – assuming that any forces so deep in Sinai must be hostile – mistakenly strafed, rocketed, and inflicted casualties upon the 7th Armored Brigade detachments that had inoperative signaling devices. A similar story unfolded for Adan at Abu Uwayulah, where IAF success combined with IAF friendly fire. Israeli jets struck the 10th Egyptian Infantry Brigade traveling from al-Arish to the Hedgehog as these troops approached Adan's battalion. Unaware, however, that friendly forces had already overrun Abu Uwayulah, IAF planes also struck Israeli armor.

The 7th Armored Brigade captures Ruafa and Egypt evacuates the Hedgehog

East of Abu Uwayulah, the al-Arish road angles towards the Hedgehog, traversing a broad, mile-long valley. To the south arises Jebel Dalfa, site of Egyptian firepower including 10 Archer anti-tank guns, seven 57 mm guns, six 25-pounder artillery pieces, two 30 mm cannon, and a handful of 40 mm Bofors and Czech 57 mm guns. This road then approaches Ruafa ridge, home to a lone Egyptian company, the only remnant of the 12th and 17th Infantry Battalions, which had redeployed to Umm Qataf.

To storm Ruafa Adan partitioned his battalion: two armored groups and one armor-infantry composite. He ordered Major Moshe Brill's Super-Sherman detachment to hit northeast Ruafa while the composite formation struck from due north. To cover these units, he directed the second armored group to shell Ruafa from a nearby knoll. Adan also arranged artillery support to guard his rear against the 10th Egyptian Infantry Battalion. Adan's Ruafa onslaught began in twilight on 31 October. Brill's Super-Shermans took immediate Egyptian fire. Chaos accompanied the composite force, which appeared half an hour later. For hours, attacks and counterattacks roiled across Ruafa ridge. Flames from blazing equipment stores and ammunition depots cast a flickering light across the heights. Having already exhausted their rounds, Super-Shermans striking northeast Ruafa functioned primarily as mobile platforms for Israeli troops in their close-quarters fighting with the Egyptian company atop the ridge. Eventually every Israeli tank involved in this struggle succumbed to Egyptian fire, but Adan and his battalion prevailed nonetheless. Numerical and vehicular superiority, and night-fighting prowess, gave Adan an edge after an eight-hour battle. By dawn, Israel controlled Ruafa.

What seemed a real breakthrough for Israel merely enraged Dayan, who hoped to occupy Ruafa and Umm Qataf by sunrise on 1 November. His wrath was again directed at Gudir, the 10th Infantry Brigade having repeatedly failed at Umm Qataf despite several advantages. Adan's assault at Ruafa distracted enemy forces, and darkness concealed Israelis approaching Umm Qataf. Perhaps most significantly, the 37th Armored Brigade (minus one of its battalions) now supported Gudir. None of these factors propelled the 10th Infantry Brigade to victory. Poor navigation doomed the unit, which became lost east of Umm Qataf. Disoriented infantrymen wandered in darkness, and when units arrived at their objective shortly before daybreak on 1 November they withdrew almost immediately.

The 10th Infantry Brigade's futile peregrinations disrupted a night punch that Dayan hoped would shatter Umm Qataf. Like Marlborough at Blenheim and Napoleon at Austerlitz, he sought a flank distraction in preparation for a central knockout blow from the 37th Armored Brigade. But this attack failed as well when the unit attacked across a minefield without armored support. Lacking tanks – a natural choice to assault fortified positions – the initial wave disintegrated, accomplishing nothing while sustaining nearly a hundred casualties, including Brigade Commander Colonel Shmuel Golinda. Umm Qataf remained in Mutawally's possession.

Fighting resumed at dawn on 1 November. After replacing Gudir with future Israeli chief-of-staff Colonel Israel Tal, Dayan again ordered the 10th Infantry and 37th Armored Brigades into action at Umm Qataf. Between the Hedgehog and al-Qusaymah Dayan deployed the 4th Infantry Brigade. Intense combat ensued. French aircraft joined Israel in showering Egyptian forces with napalm, rockets, and bombs. Armor accompanying the 4th Infantry Brigade attacked the al-Qusaymah track along Umm Qataf's southern periphery. Israeli armor again failed, suffering heavy losses and retreating around noon.

This thrust, though failing at Umm Qataf, contributed to Mutawally's decision to contract into the Hedgehog's remnants. Facing heavy pressure from every flank but the north, he abandoned all terrain except Umm Qataf and Umm Shihan. Israeli forces, facing no hostile fire from the Hedgehog's southern and eastern approaches, tightened their siege. Supply shortages complicated Mutawally's deteriorating situation. Although fighting had raged at the Hedgehog for only 48 hours, water and ammunition were too low for sustained Egyptian resistance. Ruafa Reservoir held water during spring; otherwise the Hedgehog depended on external sustenance. Apparently assuming such arrangements would continue indefinitely, no one stockpiled water. Widespread thirst resulted.

The deficiency became immaterial late on 1 November. Nasser's general withdrawal order, promulgated nearly 24 hours earlier, at last reached the Hedgehog. Mutawally and his troops had three options. The most obvious, a retreat through dunes adjoining the Hedgehog's northern flank, had serious drawbacks. Foremost among these was the risk of death by exposure, as troops with no provender stumbled across sandy wastes. However, other choices – surrendering, or attempting to break through Israeli lines at Ruafa then withdrawing along the al-Arish road – were worse.

Once darkness fell, the Hedgehog garrison therefore headed north from the Hedgehog, evacuating before midnight on 1 November. Some Egyptians died in the desert, some became Israeli prisoners, while others rejoined the 3rd Infantry Division at al-Arish. This city, the site of Egyptian headquarters in Sinai, was chaotic during

Mutawally's night-time retreat from the Hedgehog. Twenty-four hours earlier on 1 November, a triple Israeli punch shattered Egyptian positions along the northern axis and in Gaza. This area's importance as a *fedayeen* base compelled Dayan to make this thrust a centerpiece of Kadesh. Egyptian positions at al-Arish 39km (12 miles) west of the international boundary were unsuitable as an initial objective for Israeli troops, which therefore converged on Rafah astride the junction of Egypt, Gaza, and Israel.

Reducing Rafah and Sharm el-Sheikh

Preparing for combat: Israel deploys along Rafah Salient

For Israel, Rafah was doubly important. The city commanded eastern approaches to the northern axis leading to al-Arish and al-Qantarah. Also, controlling Rafah meant domination of the entire Gaza Strip, given its location at the Strip's base. Cleaving Gaza from Sinai would give Israel a free hand in destroying Gaza's *fedayeen*. Thus Dayan designated two units, the 1st Infantry Brigade, commanded by Colonel Benjamin Givli, and the 27th Armored Brigade, commanded by Colonel Haim Barlev, to storm Rafah. Facing them was Brigadier General Jaafar al-Abd and his reinforced Egyptian brigade, the 5th Infantry Brigade of the 3rd Infantry Division, with its six battalions – which included some Palestinian units – along with artillery and anti-tank batteries and a Sherman squadron. In reserve at Rafah itself was the 87th Palestinian Infantry Brigade of the 8th Palestinian Division. Al-Abd deployed some of his force five miles south of Rafah, where the borders of Israel, Egypt, and Gaza converge.

Favorable topography transformed this apex, Rafah Salient, into a strong, though shallow, defensive zone presenting no obvious avenues for attack. Dunes protected its southern flank, while 18 small hills in the salient's center and north provided high ground and concealment for Egyptian

troops, numbering slightly more than one battalion. Trenches and bunkers studded these knolls, while barbed wire, fences, and mines impeded assaults against them. To the south, where this broken country flattened, parallel minefields stretched nearly a dozen miles, abutting the northern fringe of dunes. Al-Abd deployed a battalion in this southern zone. He positioned the remainder of the 5th Infantry Brigade in an armed camp between Rafah and the road to al-Arish. Here, in tandem with the 87th Palestinian Infantry Brigade, they acted as reserves, supporting each flank as necessary against Israeli attacks.

To defeat Rafah, Dayan employed multiple spearheads, with three sequential attacks over a single night. After crashing through Egyptian defenses, each prong had the same geographical objective, a point known as Crossroads 12, 5 km (three miles) west of Rafah Salient. Converging here encircled not only Rafah but all Gaza as well, enabled armor attacks along the northern axis, and gave Israel control of local roads. In blitzkrieg fashion, Dayan instructed his units to focus on attaining and exploiting a breakthrough, rather than tediously reducing each enemy strongpoint. He knew Israeli forces could mop up after routing the Egyptian Army in Sinai.

Dayan provided similar striking power to each sector. Against the south and its triple swath of minefields directly adjacent to the border, he allocated two battalions of the 1st Infantry and an engineer contingent responsible for penetrating minefields and elaborate Egyptian defenses such as bunkers and trenches. Dayan positioned two additional infantry battalions, also of the 1st Infantry, in the center. Finally, he designated a battalion of the 27th Armored Brigade to lead the Israeli advance in the north.

Israeli patrols began probing before H-Hour, although efforts to maintain secrecy complicated their task. After darkness fell on 30 October, engineers stole into Egypt, scouting minefield channels that Israeli troops could cross during their forthcoming attack. As the engineers concluded their dangerous work, Dayan became concerned about high Israeli casualties when Group 77 attacked Rafah. He implemented schemes to attain objectives while minimizing losses. To distract Egyptian forces, Dayan scheduled his attack to start after Revise Phase I. At dusk, 13 hours behind schedule, French and British bombers appeared over Cairo. Since Dayan intended to strike after nightfall regardless, this delay had no significance at Rafah. With bombing underway, he ordered the 1st Infantry Brigade and the 37th Armored Brigade to attack. Another measure involved augmented firepower. Preceding Group 77's assault, Dayan arranged for IAF and French naval bombardment, but neither performed to his satisfaction. France's naval "sprat," as Dayan derisively called it, only hit Egyptian reserves. Israeli planes, confused in darkness, proved a double liability, illuminating then bombing Israeli troops. An angry Dayan sent these aircraft away.

Attacks at Rafah Salient: 31 October /1 November

More successful but nonetheless imperfect that night were the 1st Infantry engineers probing the southern flank. Mine detection and removal in darkness made for narrow, imperfect paths as became clear two hours before midnight on 31 October. Lieutenant Colonel Meir Pilavsky's formations of the 1st Infantry Brigade entered Egypt using these gaps. His lead units sought Hills 2 and 6. Trailing units, including another of the 1st Infantry battalions, were to capture Hills 5, 8, 10, and 293. Having gained these points, Pilavsky's battalions would rendezvous with other units at Crossroads 12.

Egyptian fire soon fractured this attack, disabling several tanks; others became lost. Individual soldiers threaded through minefields on foot, but Pilavsky's challenge was to steer tanks, which he needed for subsequent attacks on Egyptian fortifications, through narrow un-mined passages. Artillery pounded his battalion as it groped for safe passage. Perseverance ultimately prevailed. Pilavsky's battalion reached a key road shortly before dawn, turned towards Crossroads 12, and flanked

Egyptians defending Hills 5, 8, and 10. Eleven hours after entering Egypt, Pilavsky accomplished his mission. His battalion suffered two killed and 22 wounded.

Further north, Israeli objectives were Posts 25, 25A, 27, and 29. Against 29 (the key to Rafah Salient) and 27, Dayan sent a battalion, which suffered light casualties in accomplishing both missions shortly after dawn, skillfully using half-tracks against wire-lines and trenches at 29 and teaming with Shermans at 27. Posts 25 and 25A posed more problems. Poor night navigation through complex terrain challenged the 1st Infantry. An attacking battalion sought to sow confusion by appearing to surround 25 and 25A but merely confused Israeli units. Simultaneous raids on both posts failed when the company responsible for striking 25A became lost in darkness, instead assaulting 25, 50 meters east, just as another Israeli company arrived. Israeli troops somehow avoided shooting each other. These forces then stormed 25A, dispersing Egyptian soldiers into the night. Israeli casualties were six killed, most from long-range artillery.

On Rafah's northern flank, Dayan originally planned to deploy the 27th Armored Brigade at dawn on 1 November. AMX-13s and Super-Shermans would attack Posts 34 and 36 anchoring Rafah's left. Updated intelligence reports persuaded Dayan to strike earlier, although he restrained this armored punch until after midnight, as Israeli aerial and French naval bombardments ran their futile course. AMX-13s and their attached infantry achieved more success than the Super-Shermans, although both attacks started slowly. The IAF's failure to destroy Egyptian gun positions left in place much resistance to ground attacks. As motorized detachments crossed open ground just beyond the border two hours before sunrise, enemy artillery bracketed them. Incoming rounds inflicted nearly 100 casualties, including several officers.

Conditions rapidly improved, however. Infantry encircled and rocketed both 34 and 36, opening the way for AMX-13s, which

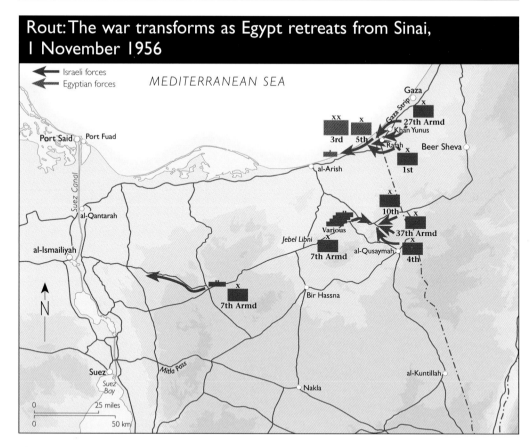

Rout: The war transforms as Egypt retreats from Sinai, 1 November 1956

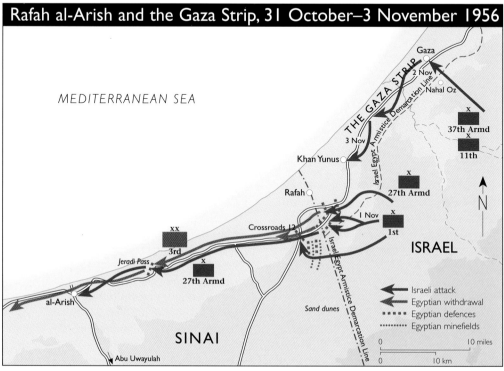

Rafah al-Arish and the Gaza Strip, 31 October–3 November 1956

sped across exposed terrain smashing Egyptian defenses. After a three-hour fight and heavy Israeli casualties, the 27th Armored Brigade now controlled Rafah's northern flank, having isolated Gaza from Sinai. Barlev's AMX-13s and Super-Shermans hardly paused, racing for Crossroads 12 where they arrived at 09:00 am on 1 November. Now armored spearheads could begin the advance on al-Arish, Sinai's most important city, while Givli consolidated control of Gaza.

Group 77's achievements at Rafah Salient, though impressive – all goals in hand and only a little behind Dayan's timetable – were incomplete since enemy troops and their equipment largely avoided capture despite chaos in Egypt. Twice during Salient battles Nasser ordered an immediate withdrawal. Al-Abd ignored the first dispatch, but complied with the second, which arrived shortly after dawn on 1 November. Despite heavy pressure on three flanks, he extracted from Rafah what remained of the 5th Infantry Brigade just two hours before Israeli infantry and armored prongs met at Crossroads 12. Thus these pincers closed on air, al-Abd having escaped encirclement.

The 27th Armored Brigade advances through Jeradi Pass to al-Arish

Undaunted by the failure to surround al-Abd's troops, Dayan directed Barlev to assemble and dispatch towards al-Arish three columns from the 27th Armored Brigade, each with infantry and artillery support. Because of their speed, a dozen AMX tanks led; Super-Shermans and AMXs followed in two groups. Dayan hoped to capture al-Arish by nightfall on 1 November. The AMX vanguard rolled west from Crossroads 12 that morning, leaving roughly six hours to cross 40 km (25 miles). In favorable conditions, this pace seemed attainable. However, Dayan's schedule failed to account for Egyptian resistance along the al-Arish road.

During the daylight hours of 1 November, most of the 3rd Egyptian Infantry Division was either retreating towards the Suez Canal or preparing to do so at sunset. Small 4th

Infantry Brigade detachments meanwhile covered the withdrawal to al-Qantarah. Al-Qadi concentrated his rearguard near al-Arish, which meant that the 27th Armored Brigade at first met little resistance. At Sheikh Zuweid, an outpost six miles from Crossroads 12, Israeli tanks found only smoking rubble, the aftermath of Mystere and Ouragan raids. As Barlev's armor closed on al-Arish, fighting intensified with a major battle erupting at Jeradi Pass. Here geography assisted an Egyptian infantry company contesting Barlev's advance. East of Jeradi a wide coastal plain allowed attacks across a broad north–south swath. The pass itself confined travel to a narrow gap, limiting Barlev's options by complicating any attempt to bypass it from the flanks or rear. Attacking on a thin front blunted 27th Armored Brigade's numerical edge, so Israeli commanders evaluated options. A minor road angling southeast to northwest from southern Rafah Salient penetrated sand dunes south of Jeradi Pass. This track offered the prospect of encircling the pass; Group 77's initial orders entailed such a maneuver. According to this plan, after Israeli forces entered southwest Gaza, the 27th Armored Brigade's reserves were to outflank Egyptians at Jeradi Pass via the secondary road as Barlev's main body approached from the east.

This plan had theoretical merit. But a delayed breakthrough at Rafah and logistical deficiencies forced Barlev to abandon elaborate maneuvers at Jeradi Pass. However, he used indirect tactics on a small scale once his vanguard arrived at a defended ridge just east of the pass. Several AMX-13s hooked left, storming its summit. Since Egyptian artillery and infantry remained on a steep eastern face, blocking movement to al-Arish, Barlev ordered air strikes. These blows, though powerful, failed to neutralize the hill, but a two-pronged armored assault hard on the heels of this aerial onslaught broke enemy positions, sending Egyptians scrambling west. Dusk, only two hours away once the 27th Armored Brigade had secured the pass, persuaded Barlev to lunge at al-Arish. A Sherman cohort advanced before accurate Egyptian artillery fire forced a twilight halt.

Chaos for Egypt's 3rd Infantry Division: Retreating to Suez

During the night of 1/2 November, while the 27th Armored Brigade prepared to attack al-Arish the following day, al-Qadi's 3rd Infantry Division retreated en masse. Those fortunate enough to survive the carnage at Rafah and Gaza scampered west, hoping to reach al-Qantarah – 160 km (100 miles) distant along the Canal – while darkness prevailed. Thus shrouded, the shattered division might avoid the Israeli air raids that made daytime travel perilous.

Also retreating that night were Egyptians fleeing the Hedgehog. Mutawally's evacuation proceeded according to plan, probably because his scheme and expectations were simple: escape Umm Qataf and Umm Shihan undetected. Unaware of the 3rd Infantry Division's grave situation, barefoot soldiers from the 6th Egyptian Infantry crossed dunes and desert, essentially defenseless but nonetheless seeking friendly units at al-Arish. In this quest, one battalion – the 18th–succeeded, while remnants of the 12th and 17th Battalions failed because of navigational shortcomings. Mutawally himself found safety among local tribes near the Hedgehog.

Mutawally's interval of secrecy exceeded Egyptian expectations. Near noon on 2 November, Israeli aircraft reconnoitering the Hedgehog noted its peculiar calm. The 37th Armored Brigade's Shermans subsequently ascended to Umm Shihan. Finding nothing, the tanks rolled west towards Ruafa; en route they encountered an ambush that the 7th Armored Brigades had laid for Egyptian troops. Most of the unit was far west, chasing T-34s and SU-100s of the 1st and 2nd Egyptian Armored Brigade as these vehicles fled to al-Ismailiyah from their earlier Sinai concentrations. However, a squadron stayed behind, assuming, in the absence of contrary information, that tanks driving west from Umm Shihan must be hostile. Their rounds struck eight of the nine

Israel captured several Egyptian prisoners after conquering al-Arish. (Topham Picturepoint)

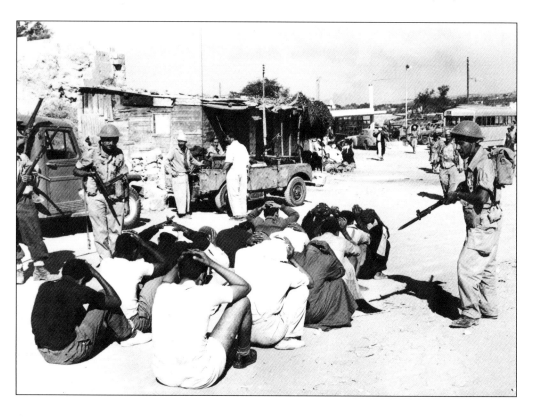

Shermans from the 37th Armored Brigade, killing its squadron commander and inflicting several other casualties.

This friendly fire marred an otherwise triumphant day for Dayan's forces. At dawn Barlev captured al-Arish, all defenders having withdrawn the previous night. The 7th Armored Brigade eventually overtook Egyptian armor in western Sinai, destroying three tanks and capturing one. Perhaps most encouraging of all in terms of overall priorities in Kadesh, 2 November represented a day of impressive success in Gaza.

Settling scores in Gaza: Israel conquers the Strip

Once al-Abd's Rafah Salient collapsed, severing Gaza from Egypt, Israeli forces prepared to overrun the Strip in its entirety. Attacks from Gaza – an Egyptian "bridgehead [across] Sinai," in Dayan's view – had long troubled Israeli leaders. Capturing this area from Egypt meant elimination of the bridgehead. Egypt based its Gaza defenses on the Strip's two major population centers, Gaza City and Khan Yunus, so Israel directed its military campaign against these settlements. Defending Gaza City was an Egyptian National Guard Brigade – 3500 troops strong – and several mortar detachments. Nearby was a small force from the Motorized Border Patrol.

A dozen miles southwest, three battalions of the 86th Palestinian Infantry Brigade and artillery units protected Khan Yunus. Against these two brigades, Dayan sent two battalions of the 11th Infantry Brigade and a 37th Armored Brigade battalion, whose half-tracks and six Shermans had not fought at the Hedgehog with the rest of their brigade. The armored battalion's main role at Gaza was as a mobile strike force, collapsing enemy defenses so that the 11th Infantry Brigade could occupy the Strip and join the 1st Infantry Brigade at Rafah.

Israel first attacked Gaza City, which, with 50,000 inhabitants, was the largest and most strategically important of Gaza's remaining settlements. Fortified hills just outside the city dominated the area. One of these, Ali Muntar, the site of a protracted

British–Ottoman World War I battle, received Egyptian machine guns and artillery. Its trenches and mines lent defensive strength. Along Ali Muntar's eastern edge, a path linked Gaza City to Beer Sheva and served as the primary avenue of attack for the 37th Armored Brigade, which struck at dawn on 2 November.

The 11th Infantry Brigade trailed the lead Shermans. When Kadesh began, one battalion from the brigade had dispersed, patrolling to intercept Egyptian and Palestinian commandos seeking to attack Israel. Therefore, late on 1 November when Israeli GHQ ordered an immediate advance against Gaza City, the 11th Infantry Brigade required time to position its units to attack the Gaza City–Beer Sheva road.

The armored battalion succeeded despite attacking without infantry support. Israeli Shermans rolled past Ali Muntar and Egyptian National Guardsmen positioned along the road. Upon penetrating Egyptian defenses, these tanks ignored resistance, speeding directly into Gaza City itself. After overrunning it, the armored team turned north, again without halting en route to engage Egyptian forces. The Shermans and half-tracks soon arrived in Bet Hanun, a mile from the Gaza Strip's northern terminus. To the 11th Infantry Brigade, now concentrated, fell the assignment of destroying the National Guard Brigade on Ali Muntar and elsewhere in Gaza City.

By noon on 2 November, Israel controlled the city, so the 11th Infantry Brigade and armor from the 37th Armored Brigade pivoted south, engaging Arab forces at Khan Yunus. Although this had fewer defenders than Gaza City, they resisted Israeli attacks when these developed on 3 November. Dayan, who hoped to capture all Gaza by dusk on 2 November, favored a faster tempo, but logistical weakness prevented rapid success. An 11th Infantry Brigade battalion was available to advance immediately into southern Gaza, but Dayan demurred. This delay indicates his growing belief in armor's importance, and was a justifiable decision in light of a tough four-hour melee that ensued at Khan Yunus the following day. This battle had two phases, the first lasting longer and having more significance than the second.

In the first stage along a defensive perimeter surrounding Khan Yunus, Israeli armor was paramount. The 86th Palestinian Brigade was sheltered within minefields, wire, and heavy-weapon strongpoints nearly impervious to infantry assault. The 37th Armored Brigade's Shermans assailed this boundary, using their firepower to blast holes in Palestinian defenses. The perimeter's collapse concluded the first battle phase and inaugurated the second, within Khan Yunus. Shermans and half-tracks accompanied the 11th Infantry Brigade's soldiers who stormed gaps in the wire and attacked Palestinian positions from flank and rear. This onslaught, which concluded around noon on 3 November, ended organized Arab defense of the Gaza Strip, although Palestinian bands remained holed up throughout Khan Yunus.

Minor firefights erupted when Israeli security forces endeavored to uproot these holdouts, but the 11th Infantry Brigade, with more pressing matters at hand, advanced six miles southwest to Rafah. Here the unit joined the 1st Infantry Brigade, completing Israel's conquest of Gaza after a 58-hour campaign. During its combat operations, the 11th Infantry Brigade suffered approximately a dozen killed and five dozen wounded.

Operation Yotvat: Israel overwhelms the Tiran Straits

Once the 1st and 11th Infantry Brigades converged at Rafah, a single Israeli strategic goal remained: the Tiran Straits. Israel's situation as of 3 November seemed quite favorable – three objectives in hand (Gaza, al-Arish, and the Hedgehog) with one to accomplish. Yet various factors cast a pall over this apparently promising scene. First, opening the Straits was Israel's most important objective. Dayan labeled it Kadesh's "primary aim." The campaign as a whole would fail if this goal was not achieved. Also, the time available for military operations in southern Sinai was shortening:

Israel could disregard the United Nations General Assembly ceasefire resolution of 1 November for only so long, and with each passing day world opinion hardened against continued fighting. Finally, and perhaps of greatest importance, the Sharm el-Sheikh campaign posed operational difficulties.

Primary among these was logistics. The Aqaba axis had no paths suitable for large, mechanized military forces, forcing the 9th Infantry Brigade, Colonel Abraham Yoffe commanding, to advance off-road nearly 322 km (200 miles) through rough country. After negotiating this maze Yoffe was to capture Sharm el-Sheikh. The 9th Infantry Brigade joined battle early in Kadesh, storming Ras an-Naqb on 30 October, then halting. Dayan, fearing Egyptian air attacks might devastate the brigade along the Aqaba

OPPOSITE   1) 27th Israeli Armoured Brigade captures al-Arish at dawn, 2 November.
2) 9th Israeli Infantry Brigade captures Ras Nasrani the afternoon of 4 November, and captures Sharm el-Sheikh the morning of 5 November.
3) 6th Egyptian Infantry Brigade withdraws to al-Arish the night of 1 November and early morning of 2 November.
4) 11th Israeli Infantry Brigade and a battalion of 37th Israeli Armoured Brigade capture Gaza City on the morning of 2 November, conquer all Gaza Strip north of Gaza City by evening, 2 November and capture Khan Yunus on the morning of 3 November.
5) Two companies of 202nd Israeli Paratroop Brigade capture Tor via airborne assault, evening of 2 November. 202nd Paratroop Brigade reaches Tor on 4 November and sets out for Sharm el-Sheikh on 4 November, reaching the city early in the afternoon of 5 November.
6) Near mid-day 2 November a squadron of 7th Israeli Armoured Brigade mistakenly ambushes 37th Israeli Armoured Brigade.
7) 3 Para (British) conducts airborne assault at Port Said's Gamil airfield the morning of 5 November. The company advanced east to the Coast Guard barracks on the afternoon of 5 November before withdrawing to the sewage works that evening.
8) 2nd Regiment Parachutiste Coloniaux (French) conducts airborne assaults of 5 November: 8:00 am in southern Port Said and 1:00 pm in Port Fuad.
9) 3 Commando Brigade (British) assaults Port Said, 6 November. 40 and 42 Commando strike amphibiously with support from 6 Royal Tank Regiment, while helicopters airlift 45 Commando to the city. 3 Commando Brigade and 6 RTR reach al Cap when the UN cease-fire takes effect during early morning of 7 November.

Israel secures Sinai while Britain and France invade the Canal Zone, 2–7 November 1956

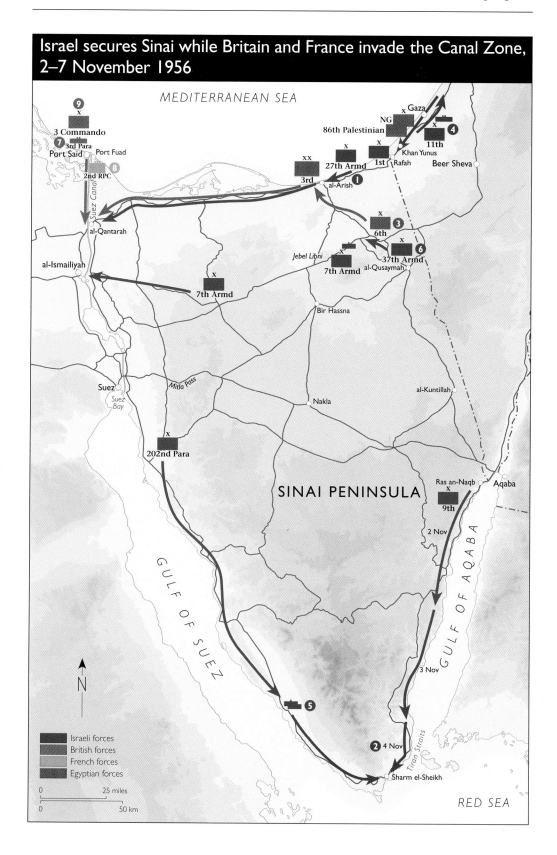

MEDITERRANEAN SEA

3 Commando
3rd Para
Port Said
Port Fuad
2nd RPC
al-Qantarah
al-Ismailiyah
7th Armd

Gaza
NG
86th Palestinian
Khan Yunus
11th
27th Armd
3rd
1st
Rafah
al-Arish
Beer Sheva
6th
Jebel Libni
37th Armd
7th Armd
al-Qusaymah
Bir Hassna

Suez
Suez Bay
Mitla Pass
Nakla
al-Kuntillah

202nd Para

SINAI PENINSULA

Ras an-Naqb
9th
Aqaba

2 Nov

GULF OF SUEZ

GULF OF AQABA

3 Nov

5

2 4 Nov
Tiran Straits
Sharm el-Sheikh

RED SEA

N

Israeli forces
British forces
French forces
Egyptian forces

0   25 miles
0   50 km

axis, waited until Britain, France, and Israel controlled Sinai's skies before authorizing any movement except patrols. Because Britain and France delayed attacking Egypt, air superiority emerged later than Dayan hoped. His Kadesh timetable – built on the Sevres schedules – stipulated a November 1 departure from Ras an-Naqb, and capture of Sharm el-Sheikh on 3 November, but the 9th Infantry Brigade left a day behind schedule.

This delay concerned Dayan, who supplemented the 9th Infantry Brigade with a second front in the form of the 202nd Paratroop Brigade, currently bivouacked near Parker's Memorial. Dayan planned to deploy these commandos against the Tiran Straits once they arrived in southern Sinai. Two alternatives were available for using Sharon's paratroops: parachuting into Sharm el-Sheikh after flying from Mitla – which Dayan preferred as the quickest option – or advancing overland from Tor on the Gulf of Suez, roughly 97 km (60 miles) by road northwest of Sharm el-Sheikh. Anti-aircraft batteries at Sharm el-Sheikh forced Israel to advance overland from Tor, an operation with two preliminary steps: advancing to and capturing the port. Dayan planned to follow this phase with an airlift, after which overland movement against Tor could begin. Airborne drops against minimal Egyptian resistance began near dusk on 2 November, and Tor's airfield was captured by nightfall.

Earlier that day, Yoffe's column left Ras an-Naqb, and trekked for 60 hours across arduous terrain. While en route, the 9th Infantry Brigade saw few enemy forces. In keeping with Nasser's order of 31 October, most Egyptians had quit Sinai. Some forces, however, including two battalions at Sharm el-Sheikh under Colonel Raouf Mahfouz Zaki, remained. Nasser intended to evacuate Zaki once naval support became available. In the short run, though, Zaki was to hold the Tiran Straits. Egyptian positions in southern Sinai had some advantages. At Sharm el-Sheikh were an airstrip, port, and extensive supplies. Bunkers, trenches, minefields, artillery, and anti-aircraft guns protected Ras Nasrani and Sharm el-Sheikh, while Ras Nasrani also had 6-inch coastal guns

sited to dominate the Tiran Straits. Ten miles west atop high ground, Jebel Aida supported both positions. However, closer examination reveals that Zaki had little chance of outright military victory; realistically he could only hope to delay defeat. In ideal circumstances, an Egyptian sea-lift would precede Yoffe's arrival.

Zaki, new to Aqaba, knew little of local conditions. He inherited positions built upon the assumption that Israel would attack Sharm el-Sheikh with paratroops. His forces included no tanks. Ras Nasrani and Sharm el-Sheikh were incapable of mutual fire support, and key immobile assets were divided between the two localities. Thus, consolidation meant sacrifice. But complete Israeli air domination was perhaps Zaki's greatest problem. Israel's warplanes provided continuous reconnaissance, whereas Zaki had little information regarding enemy movements. Complicating Zaki's situation, Israeli fighters started intense strikes against Sharm el-Sheikh in early November. These raids continued round the clock for three days.

Contemplating these Egyptian disadvantages may have lifted Yoffe's spirits; certainly he needed encouragement as he advanced on the Tiran Straits. The first 160 km (100 miles) took 30 hours. Despite efforts to travel lightly, time and again brigade vehicles lodged in sand, necessitating muscle power for a renewed advance. Their journey temporarily "eased" – a relative term – once the 9th Infantry Brigade surmounted high ground 16 km (10 miles) south of Ain al-Furtaga. However, encounters with enemy patrols increased as the Israeli column approached the Straits. Their first engagement of consequence developed on 3 November at Dhahab, a coastal Egyptian post 72 km (45 miles) north of Sharm el-Sheikh. Here a 9th Infantry Brigade patrol, commanded by Lieutenant Arik Nachamkain, encountered and routed Egyptian soldiers. When the rest of the brigade later arrived at Dhahab, Yoffe halted but Dayan, overhead in a Dakota, exhorted him to continue. At dusk on 3 November, therefore, his march resumed.

Meanwhile the 202nd Paratroop Brigade's preparations for opening a second front proceeded rapidly. After Israel seized Tor airfield on 2 November, an airlift began. Through the night of 2/3 November, Dakotas and NordAtlases ferried a battalion of the 12th Infantry Brigade into Tor. Overland from Parker's Memorial, meanwhile, came the remainder of the 202nd Paratroop Brigade, arriving at Tor late the following afternoon. Here the paratroops consolidated, departing the next day for Sharm el-Sheikh via a paved road.

After leaving Dhahab on 3 November, the 9th Infantry Brigade again encountered enemy forces, this time at Jebel Ashiri and Wadi Kid. Using terrain and darkness to maximize the effects of grenades, machine gun fire, and mines, an Egyptian platoon half-heartedly ambushed Israeli patrols. Although the Egyptian contingent inflicted few casualties and soon fled, their ambush delayed Yoffe's brigade for 11 hours. Israeli engineers eventually established safe passage through the narrow path, and at mid-morning of 4 November the convoy continued.

That noon, the 9th Infantry Brigade arrived at Ras Nasrani, northernmost of the Tiran Straits strongpoints where Nachamkain discovered that Zaki's units had fled south. Zaki, with too few men to protect both localities against a large Israeli force, decided to defend Sharm el-Sheikh and its airfield and deep-water port. The 9th Infantry Brigade therefore marched towards Sharm el-Sheikh 16 km (10 miles) south, en route winning numerous skirmishes along the outpost's northern periphery. Darkness fell before Yoffe arrived at its outskirts, but he attacked nonetheless. At midnight, two companies hit and nearly overran Egyptian positions west of the city, but retreated with heavy casualties after a four-hour assault.

Half-tracks and jeeps soon led another strike from the west – this one battalion-sized and enjoying ample firepower in the form of artillery support and air-delivered napalm – smashing Egyptian defenses around Sharm el-Sheikh an hour after dawn on 5 November. In tandem with a simultaneous advance from the east by another of the 9th Infantry Brigade's battalions, Yoffe had Zaki in a nutcracker.

Rolling barrages, in which Israeli ground forces advanced behind an air strike screen, ended Egyptian resistance. Zaki surrendered at 09:30 am on 5 November, six hours before the 202nd Paratroop Brigade arrived at Sharm el-Sheikh. Kadesh was over, although to the northwest of Sinai, Revise had hardly begun.

Egypt and France face mobility predicaments

Bombing panics Nasser so France seeks to accelerate Revise against British resistance

Dusk on 31 October found Nasser pleased with his situation. Despite earlier concerns of an Anglo-French attack, he now dismissed such thoughts. He enjoyed the advantage of fighting on a single front, Sinai, and on favorable terrain. For 48 hours his forces resisted Israeli attacks. The Hedgehog remained intact despite the 7th Armored Brigade's success at al-Dayyiqa. Quiet prevailed along the northern axis, as yet under Egyptian control. Meanwhile, darkness meant that Egyptian forces could move at will, free from devastating daytime Israeli air strikes. Although Israel gained an upper hand that day in Sinai's skies, Egypt's air force remained capable of strafing and bombing. Moreover, high morale prevailed among the Egyptian people.

Finally, all signs indicated widespread opposition to Kadesh even among Israel's allies. The United States attempted several times on 30 and 31 October to pass UN Security Council resolutions condemning Israel's invasion and demanding her withdrawal from Sinai. The Soviet Union, Egypt's ally, supported these proposals; only French and British vetoes succeeded in stemming the Security Council tide, which subsequently referred the issue to the General Assembly. These vetoes met short-term British and French needs but angered American leaders, who increasingly suspected collusion between Britain, France, and Israel.

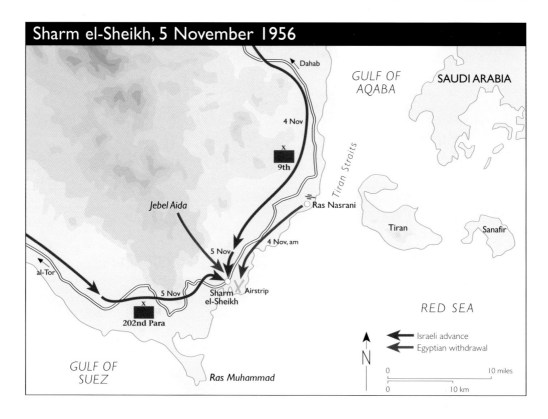

Sharm el-Sheikh, 5 November 1956

Dahab

GULF OF AQABA

SAUDI ARABIA

4 Nov

x
9th

Jebel Aida

Tiran Straits

Ras Nasrani

Tiran

Sanafir

5 Nov

4 Nov, am

al-Tor

5 Nov

Sharm el-Sheikh

Airstrip

x
202nd Para

RED SEA

N

Israeli advance
Egyptian withdrawal

0   10 miles
0   10 km

GULF OF SUEZ

Ras Muhammad

Sharm el-Sheikh. Prior to attacking this outpost, Colonel Abraham Yoffe led 9th Infantry Brigade across more than a hundred miles of rugged Sinai terrain such as the distant mountains pictured here. (Topham Picturepoint)

Lt Col P Crook and his Tac HQ move into airport buildings, El Gamil airfield, Port Said after airborne assault on 5 November 1956. (Topham Picturepoint)

After sunset, though, Nasser's exuberance collapsed in the flames of bombs exploding throughout Cairo. Britain and France would fight after all. Egypt's single front, Sinai, such an advantage only hours ago, suddenly presented a nightmare scenario. An Anglo-French invasion of the Canal Zone could envelop the Egyptian Army in a killing zone – Israeli columns from the east, British and French pincers from the west – threatening Nasser's government and Egyptian independence.

Nasser therefore summoned his military leaders, having already decided upon a withdrawal from Sinai. Opposition arose from several quarters. General Amer advocated remaining in Sinai despite the encirclement risk. He wanted Egyptian units, at that moment joined in combat, to repel Israel before leaving Sinai. Amer thought Egyptian reinforcements might favorably tip the balance at Rafah, the Hedgehog and Heitan Defile. Thus Nasser himself had to order Egypt's withdrawal. His directive came as battles raged across Sinai, and dramatically changed the situation there. His new strategy, and growing international opposition to continued hostilities in Egypt, prompted reconsideration of Revise schedules.

French commanders, bolder than their risk-averse British counterparts, proposed immediate deployments to Egypt. Well before Revise, Beaufre predicted an early Egyptian collapse and held in reserve various schemes for accelerated action. In late October his opportunity arose. On the 30th of that month, Beaufre suggested sending marines and airborne forces into the Canal Zone, but warned that this operation was only feasible if Egypt disintegrated. Subsequent discussions expanded his plan, now termed Omelette, outlining a role for British paratroops, who would capture Gamil airfield west of Port Said. Meanwhile Royal Marines, traveling by helicopter, would occupy bridges spanning Junction Canal at Raswa. Additional Canal Zone drops would secure Anglo-French control of Suez. Omelette had limitations. Its shortage of firepower – in particular, no armor – probably meant success only if Egypt mustered no Canal Zone resistance. Accordingly Beaufre contemplated circumstances in which Egypt continued to fight. In these conditions he favored an amphibious assault, but the allied armada remained far from Egypt. To save time he proposed that this armada proceed directly to Port Said without visiting Cyprus, but Task Force commanders refused.

Strategic developments added impetus to the French preference for attacking Port Said straightaway. Aware that Egypt neared collapse as its troops retreated across Sinai, Beaufre and French political leaders urged immediate action. But amphibious attacks remained several days off, as the allied convoy sailed across the Mediterranean. So long as Egypt maintained some Canal Zone presence – meaning at least several more days as retreating units withdrew from Sinai – Omelette entailed unacceptable risk. Therefore, Beaufre tinkered, hoping to hasten schedules even if Egyptian resistance continued. He developed a new proposal, Omelette II, which the Task Force commanders rejected. Their opposition to paratroop deployments where immediate reinforcement was impossible continued. Other French commanders faced an equally galling situation. The British chiefs rejected French chief-of-staff Paul Ely's request for immediate airborne raids against Egypt, and vetoed other schemes such as Israeli assistance or using warships to ferry marines to Egypt more quickly.

Increasing prospects for success in Egypt, combined with a pending UN General Assembly session, prompted Beaufre to develop new plans, which on 3 November gained British approval. His creation, Telescope (sometimes called Simplex), differed from Omelette II only in timing – its assaults took place 24 hours before Revise Phase III. Keightley and Stockwell overcame their conservatism and approved Telescope, although international and domestic pressure to cease hostilities forced Eden to restrict it. He agreed to deploy a day early while stipulating that allied forces must fight only along the Canal Zone.

On 4 November, French and British commanders refined Telescope, transforming it into Telescope Modified. British fears about helicopter vulnerability to anti-aircraft fire gave France responsibility for Raswa operations, for which French leaders selected a parachute assault. But Raswa's difficult terrain – small, with adjoining water – made airborne operations quite problematic. Dispersion doomed French paratroopers to certain defeat, but Generals Jacques Massu (10th Parachute Division commander) and Jean Gilles assured Beaufre that their forces could hit a small drop zone. This assessment appealed to Beaufre, who wanted a significant French role on 5 November. More importantly, Beaufre believed that the bridges constituted the key objective in Port Said. In spanning Junction Canal, they allowed armor to travel the Canal road. If Egypt destroyed or otherwise denied Raswa to French and British forces, Port Said became a dead-end, precluding any land-based exploitation until allied engineers erected pontoons across Junction Canal.

Above Egypt: Britain and France pursue air supremacy

After Israel invaded Sinai, British bomber wings under the command of Group Captains G.C.O. Key and Lewis Hodges prepared for battle. Ambiguity surrounding the Arab–Israeli military situation limited them to tentative planning, but all signals indicated imminent combat operations. Initial scenarios outlined night attacks against Egypt's bomber fleet early on 31 October. On 30 October, the extent of future RAF activity gained greater clarity when British chiefs instructed Key and Hodges to institute a six-hour alert. Following Eden's parliamentary ultimatum of 31 October, the chiefs refined their guidance, ordering bombing to begin the next morning. Confusion arose among Task Force commanders. Eden deprived them of key information about the Sevres Protocol, meaning that they failed to grasp the interaction between Kadesh and Revise. Was Britain's adversary Egypt? Israel? Both? Neither? The Task Force commanders did not know.

Adding to their discomfort, Egyptian MiGs unexpectedly intercepted high-altitude RAF reconnaissance aircraft. Already wary of daytime operations with MiGs aloft, British air commanders opposed such sorties after this incident. They now wanted night bombing only, since Egyptian pilots depended primarily on visual identification. The chiefs agreed, but warned that daytime missions must begin if Egyptian bombers hit Israel. At Akrotiri half a dozen Canberras went on alert to attack Egypt if this contingency arose.

Revise Phases I and II – air supremacy and an "aero-psychological" campaign – commenced 13 hours after the Anglo-French ultimatum expired. While Nasser planned Sinai's reinforcement, seven Cyprus-based Canberras and eight Valiants from Luqa, Malta, flew to Cairo West airbase, 30 km (19 miles) northwest of Cairo and home to several Il-28 Beagles. At last the Beagles, which had flown recent sorties against Israel and elicited from Ben-Gurion a near-phobic reaction for their ability to bomb Israeli cities, appeared doomed.

However, as British bombers approached the African coast, Eden learned that American nationals were evacuating from Cairo near Cairo West. Horrified about potential American casualties, Eden ordered the Valiants to return to Malta and diverted the Canberras to Cairo's Almaza military base – home to MiG-15, Meteor, C-46, C-47, and Il-14 aircraft – which the lead jets struggled to identify and hit with their bombs. The complexities of high-altitude night precision attacks with "dumb" ordnance meant many opportunities for failure. For instance, these circumstances amplified the effect of atmospheric conditions such as wind and temperature, resulting in less accuracy. Although Phase II planners had identified Radio Cairo, a key pillar of Nasser's government, as a primary target, Eden removed it from British lists because of concern over civilian casualties. No one in the British command structure realized that Radio Cairo's transmitters were far from populated areas.

The night was not a complete failure. Bombers eventually struck Almaza, while additional sorties raided several other Egyptian bases, including Kabrit and Abu Suwayr, both home to MiG-15 squadrons, and Inchas, an occasional Beagle base. However, British bombing inaccuracy yielded disappointing results. Follow-on photographic reconnaissance indicated minor Egyptian damage, prefiguring an ineffective four-day bombing campaign. Low-altitude daytime multi-purpose fighter strikes employing visual targeting techniques attained more success than the hapless Canberra and Valiant night attacks.

British and French multi-purpose fighters destroy Egypt's air force and Phase II targets Egyptian morale

Multi-purpose fighters operating from Cyprus and allied carriers were well-suited for an air-supremacy campaign against "soft" targets – parked Egyptian aircraft. Such fighters proved ideal in conditions requiring bombing accuracy. Before dawn on 1 November, dozens of carrier-based Seahawks, DeHavilland Sea Venoms and Chance-Vought Corsairs and land-based DeHavilland Venoms and Thunderstreaks with Hawker Hunter escort flew to Egypt.

As the sun appeared in the east, these planes strafed their targets, which included the bases RAF bombers had attacked the previous night as well as Kasfareet, home to Vampire squadrons; Fayid, home to Meteor and Vampire squadrons; and Dekheila, near Alexandria. Although most Beagles had escaped to Upper Egypt, Syria, and Saudi Arabia, the fighters, bombers, and transports at these bases suffered cannon and rocket attacks. Nasser realized the magnitude of this defeat, which destroyed the vast majority of Egypt's operational force – roughly 200 planes – but his enemies did not until the following day. Canberras and Valiants returned to Egypt that night, again raiding Cairo West and other airfields, seeking to destroy an already vanquished adversary.

This successful 36-hour campaign meant difficult choices. Anglo-French forces could initiate an aero-psychological campaign per Revise Phase II and damage Egyptian morale by striking refineries and petroleum installations. Other enticing Phase II options were Radio Cairo and leaflet dispersal. Millions awaited distribution by British bombers. Alternatively, Anglo-French air forces could fight tactically and operationally. This course had appeal. Strongly negative world reaction against striking Egyptian targets primarily civilian in nature showed the risk of a lengthy strategic campaign.

Keightley and the Task Force commanders chose to bomb a range of targets. They abandoned oil facility strikes. Unexpected Middle Eastern developments forced Keightley's hand here. When Revise began, saboteurs destroyed pumping stations along a key Iraqi oil pipeline. Raids against Egyptian oil facilities might trigger additional retribution against British conduits. But Keightley pursued other Phase II activities. With pamphlets in Cyprus awaiting dispersal, and bombers capable of carrying them based nearby, leaflet distribution seemed easy to implement.

However, aircrew resistance and technical challenges soon forced Keightley to abandon the leaflet program. By contrast, the Phase II dalliance with broadcast propaganda – disabling Radio Cairo – was more successful, although it too fell short in many ways. Eden's reluctance to inflict non-combatant casualties slowed this initiative, but progress resumed when British planners learned of Radio Cairo's desert location. Since strikes could begin at once without fear of civilian deaths, 18 Canberras attacked the transmitters at high speed and low altitude during daytime. No ordnance hit the complex itself but one bomb struck an antenna, disabling Radio Cairo for several days before technicians succeeded in erecting another mast. With a monopoly over North African airwaves, the Cyprus-based Voice of the Allied Military Command warned Egyptians "we shall bomb you [wherever] you hide." These clumsy exhortations accomplished little. Egyptian listeners considered them nothing more than enemy lies.

Aero-psychological efforts give way to aerial interdiction

Multi-purpose fighters meanwhile attacked tactically and operationally, attempting to minimize resistance to Revise Phase III. Targets included armor and trucks capable of reinforcing the Canal Zone and infrastructure on which these reinforcements could travel. Allied planes pounded depots across Egypt. Seahawks and Westland Wyverns flattened Huckstep Barracks, an enormous vehicle concentration near Cairo, while other warplanes attacked military materiel at Al Maya Barracks.

Various limitations prevented all-out infrastructure attacks, since Revise depended on some infrastructure for movement. Unnecessary for Phase III, though, was a bridge connecting the Canal Zone with Dumyat, 48 km (30 miles) west, which provided a western reinforcement route for

Port Said. Therefore on 3 November many planes struck, yet failed to drop, the Dumyat span, which resisted attack after attack. Finally a swarm of rockets crumbled enough masonry to sever the road. Egypt's rail system presented another enticing target, since this web transported soldiers and weapons throughout the Canal Zone. Particularly successful were raids near al-Ismailiyah. On 3 November, Canberras broke all regional lines, marking one of the few tangible bomber contributions to the war. A day later, Valiants and Canberras flew their last Revise sorties, attacking Alexandria. Fittingly, these were a diversion; Keightley hoped to fool Nasser into moving forces to western Egypt. Phase II ended as it began – a sideshow to more consequential military developments.

As Britain and France shifted to vehicular and infrastructure targets, one deviation emerged. Eden had earlier canceled strikes at Cairo West airbase, allowing Egyptian Beagles to scatter. Some fled to Syrian and Saudi bases. Widening the war beyond Egypt repelled Eden, but some Ilyushins remained at Luxor. Its distance from Cyprus perhaps contributed to failure on the night of 2 November: Canberras attacked but inflicted no damage. Britain unwisely continued night attacks even after gaining air supremacy. RAF bombers relied primarily on visual targeting, a technique that worked poorly at night. Subsequent night raids also failed, leaving Luxor's Beagles unscathed until 4 November, when French Thunderstreaks rocketed the airbase, destroying the bombers.

These Egyptians in French custody were lucky – French soldiers in Egypt often followed a 'no-prisoners' creed. (Topham Picturepoint)

Boots on the ground: Revise Phase III

Telescope Modified: Paratroops capture Gamil, Raswa, and Port Fuad

Brigadier M.A.H. Butler, 16th Independent Parachute Brigade commander, and the 687 "Red Devils" of the 3rd Parachute Battalion Group (3 Para), Lieutenant Colonel Paul Crook commanding, formed the first wave of Telescope Modified. After waking hours before dawn, 3 Para left Nicosia aboard obsolete Hastings and Vickers Valettas. Soon their armada – 32 strong plus a Canberra B.6 to mark the drop zone – joined a French contingent of 22 NordAtlases operating from Tymbou airfield. Aboard these transports were Lieutenant Colonel Pierre Chateau-Jobert and his men of 2e RPC, a small British contingent, and a French special forces unit.

British paratroops patrol Port Said after the United Nations cease-fire. Sporadic violence erupted in the city until Britain and France withdrew in December 1956. (TRH Pictures)

Preceding the airlift convoy over Port Said were two dozen ground-attack aircraft. These and other French and British planes loitered all day, first pounding drop zones, then, once paratroops landed, responding to air support requests. The airlift convoy meanwhile droned towards Egypt, splitting two hours after leaving Cyprus. En route to their Junction Canal objective, the NordAtlases peeled away from their British counterparts, while Hastings and Valetta pilots tracked a smoke beacon marking their drop zone. Clear and calm weather heralded ideal jump conditions.

British and French paratroops had several objectives, foremost among them seizing Canal Zone territory before hostilities ended. As United Nations ceasefire talks were to resume on 5 November after a four-day respite, the issue figured prominently in Anglo-French political and military circles. For Ely, Barjot, Eden, and others, placing boots on the ground provided a valuable bargaining chip in subsequent negotiations concerning the Suez Canal's future.

Red Devils aboard their transports 5 November 1956. That day they flew from Cyprus to Egypt and just after dawn parachuted into Port Said. (TRH Pictures)

Related to this objective was an interest in probing Egyptian strength in and around Port Said. Prior to Telescope Modified, Butler informed his military superiors that 3 Para could, in a single day, capture not only Gamil airfield, but Port Said's harbor complex as well. Securing this prize eased British and French logistics by allowing cumbersome armor and lorries to offload directly at port. Events may have vindicated Butler had his entire brigade attacked on 5 November. However, constraints on the space available for tactical airlift at Cyprus limited the Gamil assault to a single battalion.

Another significant objective focused on infrastructure. Near Raswa lay the municipal waterworks, on which Port Said, built on brackish swamps, depended entirely. Seizing it provided leverage against the city, which Britain and France could use to their advantage. Also,

as the Allies planned to occupy Port Said indefinitely, protecting its water supply against Egyptian sabotage was important.

Finally, Telescope Modified focused on the potential advantages of Gamil's dual airstrips. British occupation denied them to Egypt while allowing their use by Anglo-French planes. However, Egypt's air force collapsed before 5 November, while Gamil's limited size prevented its use by most RAF planes. Gamil, therefore, lacked much air power significance.

Gamil's long, narrow profile – Mediterranean Sea to the north, Lake Manzala to the south, and little intervening land – allowed only two drop-zone flight paths for Hastings and Valetta pilots: east or west. Both options had disadvantages. An eastern approach subjected their vulnerable, low-flying planes to Port Said anti-aircraft fire, while a western approach meant staring into a rising sun.

Once over a drop zone nearly five miles west of Port Said, 3 Para exited their aircraft

ABOVE   Operation Telescope Modified: French paratroops in their Port Said drop zone, the morning of 5 November 1956. (Topham Picturepoint)

BELOW   British Red Devils in Cyprus. These paratroops parachuted into Port Said on 5 November, opening the ground phase of Operation Revise. They seized Gamil airfield but darkness and Egyptian resistance prevented capture of Port Said's harbour. (Topham Picturepoint)

with several objectives. A Company assaulted Gamil's control tower and western end, B Company attacked the east, and C Company sought the airfield's center. Air contact teams – observers who arranged aerial and naval support – accompanied these three units. Under canopy, all British formations came under fire. Before Telescope Modified, air strikes silenced some but not all Egyptian resistance at Gamil. Equipment limitations prevented British paratroops from returning fire until they landed. Fortunately for Britain, inaccurate and sporadic Egyptian fire had little effect and 3 Para suffered very few casualties.

Once on solid ground the Red Devils commenced combat operations, employing Stens, medium machine guns, three-inch mortars, and anti-tank weapons. Cargo limitations for the side-loading Hastings and Valettas meant that the paratroopers had little heavy equipment and no artillery. Later that day, 3 Para's minimal firepower of 10 impeded progress, but available equipment proved adequate to capture the airfield. Anti-tank weapons allowed rapid clearance of four concrete pillboxes, and within an

hour of landing, 3 Para captured Gamil after suffering a dozen casualties.

The battalion advanced east towards Port Said. Egyptian tactics soon became clear: Egyptian troops fought and retreated using defensible terrain to cover a methodical withdrawal while avoiding annihilation in set-piece engagements. Once 3 Para brought to bear their superior skill, Egyptian forces displaced to another area of strength. Along their line of retreat lay strong defensive zones which they used to good effect on 5 November.

During skirmishes that day, distant Egyptian SU100s attacked British troops. These vehicles fused a 100 mm gun's punch with a tank's mobility, making them effective against Anglo-French forces, yet difficult targets even for fast-moving allied aircraft. After leaving Gamil for Port Said, the paratroops took fire from an unlikely quarter when French aircraft strafed B Company. Having survived this friendly fire,

A British para at Gamil airfield, 5 November 1956, during Telescope Modified. (Topham Picturepoint)

B Company attacked Port Said's sewage works. Structures and foliage in and around this complex offered cover for Egyptian snipers who fought for an hour before retreating to a cemetery nearby.

Port Said's graveyard, though less defensible than its sewage works, nonetheless provided some protection, forcing B Company to arrange air support, and again slowing British progress. *Bulwark*-based Seahawks joined the fight; their rocket attacks drove Egyptians from their cemetery redoubts, but additional strongpoints lay east. Notable among these was the Coast Guard barracks, a formidable structure housing many armed Egyptians.

To avoid storming this defensible position in the face of withering enemy fire, B Company again arranged air support. As *Eagle*-based Wyverns approached at low level, Egyptian fire downed the lead airplane, whose pilot parachuted to safety. However, other Wyverns survived to release their 1000-pound bombs, blasting holes in the building and inflicting heavy casualties within. B Company subsequently withdrew, despite these punishing aerial attacks. Nearly a full day of fighting depleted British ammunition stocks, necessitating re-supply before any additional advance.

D Company, 3 Para, arrived at Gamil the afternoon of 5 November. Conceivably Brigadier Butler could have dispatched these troops to the Coast Guard barracks, with instructions to continue B Company's advance. Also available to fight were A and C Companies, currently defending terrain of little value. However, embarking on such operations required time; paratroops needed to assemble equipment, consolidate units, and prepare weapons. As dusk overtook Gamil, Butler decided against further offensives into Port Said. Concern over D-Day bombardment contributed to his caution; a few miles' separation from the assault beaches provided a safety margin. B Company withdrew west in the late afternoon, establishing defensive positions at the sewage works. Clouds of biting insects and a ferocious stench made for a miserable bivouac.

Sixteen km (10 miles) southeast, light Egyptian resistance and narrower French objectives than those of 3 Para allowed for more rapid success than at Gamil. Three units parachuted into Raswa, and each had different goals. 2 RPC sought the Port Said waterworks, while a special forces detachment was to capture at least one of Raswa's two bridges. The (British) Guards Independent Parachute Company went a different direction, probing the Canal road and causeway, a crucial artery for southern exploitation. By necessity this scouting mission was to be geographically limited. Otherwise allied aircraft, assuming troops any distance from Port Said must be Egyptian, might attack them. But even a short reconnaissance offered valuable intelligence.

All these units faced the challenge of hitting a tiny, triangular drop zone with water (Lake Manzala, Junction Canal, and Suez Canal) bounding every side. The drop zone's size – a few hundred yards per side – necessitated accuracy so that troops landed on terra firma. To mitigate anti-aircraft fire against the NordAtlases during their low-level runs over the drop zone, Corsairs and Seahawks flew suppression missions which succeeded in that anti-aircraft fire downed no transports, although nine planes sustained damage.

To enhance concentration the paratroops leapt much lower than minimum altitude regulations dictated. Their technique generally worked, although much heavy equipment missed the drop zone. Minimal time aloft meant fewer shots for defenders firing while the paratroops drifted to earth. Upon landing, the paratroops used local terrain as cover while units assembled their equipment and quickly overwhelmed resistance at the waterworks, cutting Port Said's supply. The special forces unit meanwhile marched to the Raswa bridges. Their running battle with nearby Egyptian soldiers damaged the eastern bridge, rendering it inoperable. However, French forces seized the western span. A potential chokepoint now lay in allied control.

Thus by mid-morning both French teams had accomplished their Telescope Modified

Reinforcing success: French paratroops in their Port Fuad drop zone, the afternoon of 5 November 1956. (Topham Picturepoint)

goals. Their breakthroughs were due to many factors including experience. Also, Anglo-French air supremacy allowed an interesting command and control technique for coordinating operations. While fighting raged, French commanders circling above in an airborne command post observed troops and terrain, allowing integration of battlefield tactics and air support. Another important reconnaissance mission was underway as well. British paratroops aboard two jeeps raced south, scouting the road to al-Qantarah as far as six miles beyond Junction Canal. Surprisingly, the road could support an allied thrust – no mines and only a few craters marred its surface. Furthermore the jeep patrols noted no Egyptian presence there.

Success at Raswa allowed aggressive follow-on paratroop deployments. If 2 RPC encountered heavy resistance at the waterworks, French commanders planned to reinforce their initial drop zone. However, in late morning, when 2 RPC accomplishments became clear, Chateau-Jobert arranged another scheme – afternoon airborne assaults into Port Fuad. He sought to protect 2 RPC's eastern flank by occupying the town's salt works directly opposite Raswa and, if this move succeeded, hoped to capture the whole of Port Fuad. Both goals lay within reach. Air support and fierce French assaults transformed the fighting at Port Fuad into a rout. Air strikes annihilated Egyptian troops attempting a cross-Canal retreat, leaving only isolated snipers to resist French occupation. Although paratroops spent another 12 hours eliminating resistance, by late afternoon on 5 November France won the battle for Port Fuad.

Britain and France seek Port Said's immediate surrender or an accelerated attack

This fact probably figured in Egypt's decision to consider surrendering Port Said as well. In late afternoon, Port Said military commander Brigadier Salaheddin Moguy requested immediate negotiations. Moguy, a recent arrival at Port Said, knew little of high-level

General Jacques Massu commanded French paratroops during Telescope Modified. His forces fought well, capturing all their objectives. (Topham Picturepoint)

Egyptian plans or local forces and their capabilities. Did Nasser prefer a fighting retreat to al-Qantarah, or perhaps a battle to the end at Port Said?

Moguy did not know, but buying time through negotiations opened an information-gathering window. He also hoped to persuade the allies to release their stranglehold on Port Said's water supply. Additionally, he thought that a temporary ceasefire would provide his troops some recovery time, and preparations for arming the local population could continue as well. In the ensuing talks Butler, Chateau-Jobert, and Massu outlined allied terms: Port Said was to be placed under an immediate curfew and all local Egyptian forces were to surrender their weapons and march to Gamil. Moguy, pursuing Fabian tactics,

requested a full day to contemplate these terms. Butler granted Moguy four hours and proposed an interim ceasefire for that interval. Butler wanted a truce to facilitate evacuation of wounded paratroops. Moguy agreed to Butler's ceasefire and left.

While Moguy attempted to contact Cairo for guidance, allied commanders considered other options for Telescope Modified. Perhaps Butler's post-parley report indicating the remote odds of an immediate Egyptian surrender fuelled their interest in accelerating schedules. By dusk on 5 November, the allied armada lay offshore, its early arrival a function of more speed than anticipated and good weather. Thus Phase III could begin immediately rather than waiting until the following day. British Admiral Manley Power proposed one possibility: Sycamore and Whirlwind helicopters were to transport the 3rd Marine Commando Brigade to Gamil, allowing a link-up with 3 Para and subsequent advance on Port Said, nullifying the planned amphibious assaults.

Beaufre, fixated as always on rapid exploitation while tending to discount attendant risk, suggested two ways of seizing the Canal Zone. First, he suggested dawn airborne drops at al-Qantarah. Now that friendly forces held Raswa, al-Qantarah exerted a magnetic appeal to Beaufre. For him, the southern terminus of the Suez causeway constituted the next logical step in allied operations; its occupation bypassed potential bottlenecks that might delay a Canal Zone break-out.

Beaufre also proposed diverting French marines from Port Fuad to Raswa, thereby saving them several hours' marching time. From Raswa, the marines could advance south along the Suez causeway and assist in capturing al-Qantarah, or relieve 2 RPC, enabling that unit to participate in other airborne operations further south. According to Beaufre, Stockwell agreed to drop paratroops at al-Qantarah, only to renege after Moguy rejected allied terms. Details of their conversation remain nebulous. Regarding other proposed modifications, however, Stockwell stated his position clearly. In no mood to modify Revise so extensively on short notice, and unwilling to shoulder additional risk for questionable gains, he vetoed these ideas.

Among other factors, attacking at dusk diminished allied fire support, a notable liability since those units assaulting Port Said – marine commandos and paratroops – were "light" by nature. Also, although night fighting concealed the movements of attacking units, rendering them less vulnerable to defensive fire, Port Said's streets and alleys were difficult to navigate in darkness. In low visibility, local inhabitants, with their knowledge of this labyrinth, had an inherent advantage over attacking forces. Furthermore, regarding Admiral Power's proposal, helicopters had never before ferried troops directly into a combat zone. Gamil itself lay in allied hands, and medical evacuation via helicopters was ongoing, but enemy fire from its periphery still rang out periodically. Using a novel technique in adverse conditions presented more danger than Stockwell was willing to accept; he announced that Revise's existing timetable would stand.

Nor did Stockwell want blurred lines demarcating allied amphibious zones in Port Fuad and Port Said. Thus he rejected Beaufre's plan to insert French marines directly at Raswa. His decision typifies a key difference between the Task Force commander and his French deputy. Stockwell favored existing plans; their methodical construction and underlying staff work reduced risk. Beaufre, by contrast an opportunist, saw plans as merely a means to an end, without much inherent value. For him, altered circumstances or assumptions provided adequate justification to jettison part or all of the original plan.

As Stockwell and Beaufre argued, back in Port Said Moguy contacted higher headquarters at al-Ismailiyah. Britain and France wrongly believed that all lines of communication linking the city with the outside world were gone. Nasser, lacking details about Moguy's parley but apparently aware of the ongoing talks, had no intention

of surrendering. He attempted to cashier Moguy and promote a battalion commander in his place, although confused command and control arrangements limited the effectiveness of Nasser's order. Moguy, sensing the importance of continued resistance, rejected Butler's terms at 09:30 pm on 5 November. In response, Butler proposed an hour-long ceasefire extension; Moguy, who benefited from each additional minute of ceasefire, agreed. No further extensions followed; at 10:30 pm the truce expired.

After the Suez campaign, some participants condemned Butler's decision to participate in a ceasefire, contending that it undercut allied efforts. These critics alleged that pausing operations at a time when Anglo-French forces possessed momentum and initiative curtailed opportunities for further battlefield success. This criticism is flimsy, since Butler halted 3 Para's advance for other reasons well before negotiations began. Also Anglo-French forces at Raswa, having by and large achieved their objectives and lacking manpower for additional offensive moves, had assumed a defensive mode by mid-afternoon.

Preparing Port Said's beaches for an imminent Anglo-French assault

As fighting resumed in Port Said late on 5 November, certain facts were apparent. Most importantly, despite wavering at times, Egyptian forces withstood allied paratroop landings, avoiding a rout and ignominious surrender. Their success belied Brigadier Butler's earlier optimism. Judicious exchanges of territory and time by Egyptian soldiers cheated Britain and France of a rapid tactical victory. Thus, Egypt deprived its adversaries of a logistical base at Port Said from which to advance on al-Qantarah and al-Ismailiyah. 3 Para's failure to capture Port Said and its harbor on 5 November forced Britain and France to proceed with Revise Phase III, with all its implications for casualties and damage.

In fact, the depressing prospect of shelling a city of roughly 200,000 inhabitants prompted a brief British consideration of alternative invasion sites near Port Said. Gamil presented an attractive option, since Egyptian forces could not contest a landing there. However, offshore and onshore minefields, the absence of suitable harbors, the increased distance to break-out zones at Raswa, and the general uncertainty involved with a last-minute change of plan compelled Stockwell to oppose shifting to Gamil.

For all their failures, the airborne operations yielded some benefits. French paratroops now held key parts of Port Said – its waterworks, airfield, and southern exits – and controlled Port Fuad. Moreover, despite Stockwell's decision not to land marines at Gamil, 3 Para's occupation of territory west of Port Said prevented the possibility that Egyptian forces might produce enfilading fire during landings north of the city.

As dawn approached on Tuesday morning, 6 November, smoke hung over Port Said, partially obscuring views out to sea where 1000 Royal Marines from the 3rd Commando Brigade prepared to storm a three-quarter-mile-wide beachhead immediately north of the city. After waking at 04:00 am, Lieutenant Colonels D.G. Tweed and Peter Norcock and their battalions, 40 and 42 Commando, Royal Marines, took position half a mile from the

Egyptian coast aboard *Suvla* and other Landing Ships Tank (LST). This invasion force had been at sea for nearly a week, having sailed 1,609 km (1,000 miles) from Malta during those six days.

After British and French forces parachuted into Port Said a day before, local weather deteriorated, roughening the Mediterranean to a moderate chop, but conditions remained acceptable for amphibious landings. While 40 and 42 Commando entered their ungainly "Buffalo" Landing Vehicles Tracked, Fleet Air Arm and Cyprus-based ground-attack aircraft rocketed and strafed northern Port Said to discourage Egyptian soldiers – whose numbers in the city had risen to three battalions – from resisting the imminent invasion.

Once this aerial attack ran its short but intense course, allied destroyers fired barrages, pounding not only Port Said's beach, but also a 100-meter line of wooden huts immediately adjacent to the beach. Although missing the roar of the allied fleet's largest guns – those aboard cruisers and the French battleship *Jean Bart* were absent – these salvos nonetheless struck to good effect, igniting several huts and forcing

As Port Said burns on 5 November 1956, French paratroops guard a key objective, the town waterworks. (Topham Picturepoint)

Egyptian soldiers within to abandon their breakfasts and flee inland. Cabinet-established rules of engagement for this invasion first limited gunfire to those guns 4.5 inches and smaller – thus reducing the fleet's firepower by a factor of 10 – but then, late on 5 November, prohibited any naval bombardment. The Royal Navy circumvented these restrictions through semantics. In naval parlance, "bombardment" meant "firing at targets," but another option, naval gunfire support – "firing over friendly troops at targets dangerous to those troops" – allowed British destroyers to fire landwards while adhering to the letter, if not the spirit, of their orders.

Royal Marines hit Sierra Green and Red, and establish bridgeheads: 6 November

After waiting below decks for nearly an hour, the first invasion group, roughly a fifth of 40 and 42 Commando, plunged into the Mediterranean aboard a dozen Buffaloes. These armored amphibians wallowed south, propellers churning to power them and their 20 passengers through and over the early morning chop, itself roiled from intermittent sniper fire. The burning Casino Pier illuminated the boundary dividing Sierra Red and Sierra Green, assault beaches for 40 and 42 Commando respectively. The conclusion of last-minute strafing runs indicated a temporary lull in supporting fire; 40 and 42 Commando were now alone until they could establish bridgeheads. At H-Hour, approximately 07:00 am, half an hour after leaving the relative safety of their Landing Ships Tank, Buffaloes transporting 40 Commando made landfall at Sierra Red.

Ten minutes later and some distance westwards at Sierra Green, A and B Troops, 42 Commando, lumbered ashore in their vehicles, squinting all the while to see their first objective: tall masonry buildings immediately inland of burning wooden huts. If captured, these structures offered multiple advantages. First, they functioned as a potential linchpin for strong defensive positions at the bridgehead periphery.

Furthermore, British contact teams on top of the buildings could observe Egyptian movements and direct air and naval strikes onto areas of resistance.

While A and B Troops advanced inland, an unwelcome cascade of random explosions and stray rounds showered the 150 marines, as flames from beach huts detonated ammunition caches in and beneath these blazing shacks. Enemy fire from positions west of Sierra Green also erupted sporadically. Despite this cacophony, A and B Troops succeeded in overrunning the beach huts, and soon reached a coastal road separating the beach from northern Port Said. During their advance, marines in the lead wave moved inland as quickly as possible, bypassing any resistance remaining in the swath of territory linking Port Said with its adjoining beaches. Speed and mobility were watchwords for 42 Commando during H-Hour and beyond, as the unit sought to punch a narrow hole in enemy defenses, then exploit this opening by a rapid southern advance to Port Said's strategic prizes – bridges, roads, utilities, and other key infrastructure which not only ensured control of Port Said itself, but also facilitated a break-out to al-Qantarah and points beyond. Advancing on a broad front, or pausing for clean-up operations, delayed this process, so the Royal Marines avoided these techniques.

While A and B Troops executed blitzkrieg tactics in northern Port Said, others in 42 Commando approached Sierra Green from the sea. A Landing Ships Tank shortage forced these follow-on units – C, D, E, and F Troops – to attack via Landing Craft Assault (LCA) which, unlike Buffaloes, lacked true amphibious capability. Therefore, marines in this second wave exited their craft 50 feet from shore and waded through breaking surf. As they did so, sporadic enemy fire rang out, but the diversion that A and B Troops had recently provided, together with earlier naval and aerial support, meant that the follow-on forces suffered less than they may have expected, given their lack of defensive protection. With 42 Commando's full weight now pressing against the bridgehead periphery, A and B Troops stormed through the masonry towers, spilling onto a road just beyond. 42 Commando had attained its initial objective – a defensible foothold – and further exploitation could commence. Half a mile east, 40 Commando had similar success reaching the beach and preparing for subsequent inland operations.

Marines in this assault wave had a profound advantage over their counterparts in 42 Commando: after leaving their LSTs, a dozen specially outfitted Centurions from C Squadron, 6 RTR, lumbered onto Sierra Red. In contrast to partially armored Buffaloes, which provided their occupants with only limited protection, these Centurions were invulnerable to sniping and other small-arms fire common along the assault beaches and in northern Port Said. 40 Commando made good use of the Centurions' defensive attributes and of their offensive firepower as well. After two Centurion Troops (eight tanks) drove west to join 42 Commando, 40 Commando and its attendant armor embarked on its first objective: clearing areas adjacent to Port Said's harbor. If 40 Commando succeeded, additional marine and paratroop landings – via helicopter and ship respectively – could commence. Although 40 Commando cleared a helicopter landing zone immediately inland of the port's western breakwater near a colossal statue of Canal visionary Ferdinand de Lesseps, any prospect of rapid victory receded once the marines traveled some distance down a road paralleling the waterfront.

Port Said's sprawling waterfront, including numerous basins and wharfs such as limited port facilities at the Fishing Harbor and Casino Palace Hotel, and larger quays further south at the Inner Harbor, meant that 40 Commando faced a complex clearance task. Adding to this challenge was a row of buildings along the waterfront. These structures, some massive and reinforced, provided ideal defensive positions for their occupants. At other areas in and around Port Said, Egyptian forces engaged in a fighting retreat – slow, organized withdrawal in the face of superior firepower – but along

the waterfront, Egyptians offered fierce resistance in their fortified enclaves.

Helicopters enter the fray: 45 Commando searches for an LZ

As the first such occurrence of this phenomenon raged at a police station half a mile inland, at sea on the decks of *Ocean* and *Theseus* 45 Commando prepared to reinforce their counterparts in 3rd Commando Brigade

using helicopters. No military force had ever used helicopters to airlift troops directly into a combat zone, so this experiment represented a historical milestone, and its novelty showed. Equipment and procedures each exhibited severe shortcomings. In fact, well before helicopters landed at Port Said, or even lifted off the decks of *Ocean* and *Theseus*, participants in this mobile innovation faced numerous challenges.

45 Marine commando aerially assaults Port Said via British Sycamore and Whirlwind helicopters based on HMS *Theseus* and *Ocean*, 6 November 1956. (Topham Picturepoint)

With their tiny capacity and awkward internal configuration, Sycamores and Whirlwinds of 845 Naval Helicopter Squadron and the Joint Experimental Helicopter Unit (JEHU) provided inelegant platforms for transporting ammunition-laden troops, who found themselves jammed into a small open-air cargo bay immediately aft of the cockpit. Long flights in these contorted positions could well have induced severe discomfort among passengers; thankfully for 45 Commando, *Ocean* and

Theseus were only a few minutes' flying time from Port Said.

Once airborne, another challenge appeared, in this case affecting passengers and crew. Conditions at Port Said on 6 November included fluctuating and

indeterminate front lines, dozens of burning buildings, and an ever-shifting pall of smoke due to the wind. Into this chaos flew a Whirlwind, having lifted off from *Theseus* shortly after H-Hour. Aboard was Lieutenant Colonel N.H. Tailyour, the commander of 45

Commando. These pioneers of modern warfare only just survived to recount their deeds. The helicopter's confused aircrew offloaded Tailyour at Port Said's sports stadium, still firmly under Egyptian control. In the resulting barrage of small-arms fire, dozens of rounds struck the Whirlwind before it escaped to safety with Tailyour aboard once again. Now obvious to crew and passenger alike was the need for a cleared and easily identifiable landing zone; after beating a hasty aerial retreat, they selected an area just south of Sierra Red. This landing zone, situated just southwest of the de Lesseps statue and near the Casino Palace Hotel, proved far more hospitable than the sports stadium, and the airlift of 45 Commando was on.

40 Commando facilitates reinforcement of Port Said

Near their landing zone, 40 Commando began to learn the cost in time and resources of advancing along the waterfront. Having suffered only minor casualties in smashing Egyptian resistance at Port Said Police Station, the marines slogged southwards, perhaps unaware of the difficult firefights that lay ahead. Preliminary assessments indicated that 40 Commando might secure Port Said's harbor within a few hours of its assault landing at Sierra Red, but these proved overly optimistic.

In fact, the arrival of afternoon found the marines quite a distance from the harbor's southern end, instead besieging Port Said's Customs House in an effort that proved useless until Centurions arrived and pummeled the building with short-range fire. 40 Commando soon encountered an even greater tactical conundrum upon reaching Navy House. Within this imposing edifice were over 100 holed-up Egyptians. Even flat-trajectory Centurion fire failed to dislodge the enemy. Greater firepower in

Wrecks blocking the Suez Canal prevented Britain and France from using quays in southern Port Said on 6 November, slowing their drive for al-Qantarah. (Topham Picturepoint)

Because wrecks blocked the Canal south of Port Said, British forces offload troops and equipment at locations such as the Fishing Harbour, ill-suited to the task at hand. (Topham Picturepoint)

the form of aerial rocket attacks blasted the Egyptians into quiescence, but dealing with stubborn Egyptian resistance at Navy House and other waterfront locations cost British forces casualties and time – a commodity in short supply later that day during their desperate race for al-Qantarah.

Time-consuming sieges also deprived follow-on forces of port facilities necessary for rapid debarkation, although this combat-related delay was merely one of many challenges that faced them. Dozens of capsized Egyptian blockships littering the harbor impeded Royal Navy operations. This fact became clear shortly after the

Sierra Red and Green landings when British amphibious vessels reconnoitered the harbor's northern end. Their dispatches, along with reports from the destroyers that steamed into port soon after the amphibians, foreclosed landings at Port Said's Inner Harbor, situated well south of the Canal mouth. British planners preferred landing here because of the Inner Harbor's superior facilities and the proximity to break-out zones south of Port Said.

However, north of the Inner Harbor, various unobstructed landing options existed. Foremost among these were the Fishing Harbor and the Casino Palace Hotel wharf. With some improvisation, including the use of a sea wall as an unloading platform, both proved suitable for LST operations and, by mid-morning, a stream of men and equipment left their vessels and entered Port Said. Among arriving forces were additional 6 RTR Centurions: first, tanks from A Squadron, then, roughly an hour later, from regimental headquarters and B Squadron. In their race for Raswa's bridges and al-Qantarah beyond, armored spearheads from A Squadron suffered an embarrassing setback when soft ground at the local golf links provided inadequate traction for continued movement.

Earlier on November 6, the golf course was a staging ground for unsuccessful attacks against 2 RPC at Raswa, as Egyptian forces retreated towards al-Qantarah, hoping to escape British marines pouring ashore at Port Said. Despite numerical and material disadvantages (the attackers had armor and self-propelled artillery), 2 RPC repulsed these disorganized offensives by directing Corsair strikes against Egyptian formations. Therefore few enemy remained to harass 6 RTR Centurions as they sank into the greens.

42 Commando fights through Port Said and 45 Commando exploits helicopter mobility

During a rapid southern advance, 42 Commando routed from the golf course any remaining Egyptians. Following its establishment of defensive positions at Sierra Green during mid-morning of 6 November, 42 Commando immediately expanded its bridgehead, leaving D Troop to handle any resistance. While D Troop searched masonry flats and burning beach huts for remaining Egyptians, 400 marines in five troops (A, B, C, E, and F) used Port Said's road network, particularly Shari Muhammat Ali – a major north–south thoroughfare eventually reaching the Inner Basin lock and Raswa bridges.

Port Said's Arab quarter after the United Nations cease-fire. On 5 and 6 November, shellfire and airstrikes ignited this area, most of which subsequently burned, displacing thousands of Egyptian civilians. (TRH Pictures)

Along Shari Ali lay their objectives, and within a few hours the marines accomplished them all. C Troop halted at the edge of Port Said's native district; their goal was to prevent partisan movement from redoubts in the Arab quarter to other areas of the city. They also maintained 42 Commando's lines of communication and movement along Shari Ali. Next along this road, the marines encountered the city gasworks and golf course, the latter astride not only Shari Ali, but also Shari Fuad el Auwal, Port Said's other main north–south artery.

These roads converged just north of the Raswa bridges. As 40 Commando sought to use Shari Auwal as its primary axis of advance to the bridges, by capturing the local golf course, B and E Troops of 42 Commando helped both themselves and a fellow unit in 3 Commando Brigade. A and F Troops faced minimal opposition in seizing the gasworks, allowing A and B Troops to continue their advance to Raswa. After linking with Chateau-Jobert and his paratroops they established blocking positions at the municipal electric station and awaited retreating Egyptian forces. E and F Troops stayed behind, occupying the gasworks and golf course.

As 42 Commando attained its goals one after another a far different pattern emerged than that occurring along Port Said's waterfront where 40 Commando fought fierce pitched battles against Egyptians in buildings. Objectives themselves – municipal utilities and the golf course – posed little challenge for 42 Commando, but moving between these objectives exposed the marines to snipers, who even disabled a Buffalo. Intersections posed a particular danger, since Egyptian riflemen could simultaneously pour fire onto these crossroads from four directions. The marines

adjusted by employing Centurions of C Squadron, 6 RTR, which rolled ashore at Sierra Red. While marines dashed across intersections, Centurions laid down covering fire and provided a mobile screen of armor. In addition to the challenge they posed along Shari Ali and nearby roads, irregulars also obstructed British forces elsewhere in Port Said. Responsibility for pacifying the native quarter and its innumerable insurgents lay with 45 Commando, but this clearing operation awaited the marines' arrival from their quarters aboard *Ocean* and *Theseus*. They traveled by helicopter.

Having located an acceptable landing zone south of Sierra Red, Tailyour now transported his commandos. Four assault cells, each with 120 marines aboard 22 helicopters, arrived in succession. Once the marines landed, inbound Sycamores and Whirlwinds airlifted their equipment and ammunition, while outbound craft carried allied casualties to *Theseus* and *Ocean* for treatment. During the operation, one pilot, his craft out of fuel, crashed at sea. It was the only loss for 845 Squadron and JEHU during their November 6 airlift operations, and proved insignificant to the broader campaign at Port Said.

Once 45 Commando had its gear, the marines advanced on foot along the coastal road, at right angles to 40 and 42 Commando. Almost immediately after their mid-morning departure, the marines took fire from an unlikely source. An *Eagle*-based Wyvern attacked, inflicting over a dozen casualties. Faulty procedures, in which the offshore Joint Fire Support Control Committee forwarded targeting coordinates to aircraft without consulting British air contact teams in Port Said, contributed to this incident.

Israeli commandos

Israeli commandos participated extensively in the 1956 Suez campaign. They crossed the Sinai Peninsula, fought at Mitla Pass and assisted in Israel's conquest of the Tiran Straits. In fact, the enduring IDF tenets of speed, surprise, unpredictability, and small-unit leadership arose largely from these elite forces and their mid-1950s successes.

Unconventional warfare dates back to the early years of Jewish military history. In the 2nd century BCE, the Maccabees led a successful insurgency against the Seleucid dynasty threatening Jewish religion and culture. The Maccabees used bases in the Judean wilderness to ambush enemy armies operating in Palestine. Years of hit-and-run raids eventually broke Seleucid will, leading to an independent Jewish state. Two hundred years later, during Roman domination of the eastern Mediterranean,

Jewish guerrillas again struggled against foreign occupation. The Zealots, a radical faction espousing apocalyptic beliefs and dedicated to ending Roman rule through violence, launched surprise attacks against Roman soldiers and Roman sympathizers in the Jewish community. Their goal was to plunge Palestine into anarchy and, in the ensuing chaos, seize control. Such activity helped precipitate the Jewish War, 66–70 CE, in which Roman legions sacked Jerusalem, ravaged much of Palestine, crushed Jewish resistance, and initiated the Diaspora which lasted for the next two millennia.

Early in the 20th century Zionism spurred European Jews to emigrate to Palestine, then a part of the ailing Ottoman Empire. Palestine's feudal chaos and long Islamic tradition – and consequent hostility towards Judaism – compelled these migrants upon arrival to form secret paramilitary groups such as Bar Giora and Hashomer. These covert societies primarily guarded Jewish newcomers; in this capacity they escorted Jews traveling in Palestine, sought to resolve by force land disputes in favor of Jewish claimants, and protected Jewish outposts against brigands and gangs. These paramilitaries operated defensively for the most part, although at times they operated offensively, for instance raiding villages hostile to Jewish settlement. With the onset of World War I, Ottoman security forces attempted to destroy Jewish commando bands; Hashomer and Bar Giora never recovered. Both had disappeared when Britain attained a Mandate over Palestine in the early 1920s.

In response to the Arab revolt of the late 1930s, British Captain Orde Wingate formed Anglo-Jewish Special Night Squads, training their members in hit-and-run tactics, emphasizing speed, surprise and audacity. Here Wingate inspects troops during African service. (Topham Picturepoint)

For the next 15 years, British troops maintained order. In 1936, however, Palestinian gangs seeking to undermine Britain's Middle Eastern imperialism attacked Jewish settlements and British government buildings, set ambushes, and incited urban riots with the aim of destroying British authority and forcing Zionism into retreat. Violence associated with this Arab uprising renewed traditional Jewish emphasis on commando forces, and also prompted a paradigm shift within Jewish military circles. Defensive strategies lost favor as a more offensive outlook beckoned, laying the groundwork for fundamental regional changes.

Soon after the 1930s uprising engulfed Britain's Mandate, British Captain Orde Wingate arrived in Palestine. After two years of observation he trained Jewish groups in the counterinsurgency tactics he had seen in the Sudan. His proposal for "Making His Majesty's Forces Operate at Night with the Objective of Putting an End to the Terror in Northern Palestine" resulted in the creation in 1938 of an Anglo-Jewish amalgam Wingate branded the Special Night Squads.

In keeping with the tenor of the times, these units, which totaled about 100 men, embraced offensive operations, seeking to fight behind enemy lines. As their name implied, the Special Night Squads also sought to dominate the hours of darkness. Careful intelligence, keen awareness of terrain, superior conditioning, and a flair for the unexpected completed Wingate's formula for success in low-intensity conflict. For a year, his squads struck villages suspected of harboring radicals, assassinated militant Arab leaders, and intercepted gangs bent on attacking British or Jewish targets in Palestine. Wingate left the Levant in 1939, but Special Night Squad soldiers such as Moshe Dayan perpetuated Wingate's commando legacy.

Although Israeli forces fought well in irregular warfare during the first Arab–Israeli War (1948–49), IDF special operations capabilities declined after that conflict ended. A lack of elite units capable of complex, dangerous missions, and distractions such as

the challenge of nation-building contributed to this trend. Unfortunately for Israel, such skills ebbed at an inopportune moment. Palestinians, Jordanians, and Syrians, whom the 1948–49 conflict had thrown into destitution, occasionally infiltrated across armistice lines to rob and plunder. These activities soon merged with the guerrilla tactics of Israel's neighbors, who abandoned conventional warfare, instead kidnapping, planting mines, and killing as opportunities presented themselves.

Numerous Israeli retaliations in the early 1950s, which began poorly in Syria in May 1951 and soon deteriorated to abysmal levels, illustrated the sorry state of Israeli commando capabilities. A failure at Falema, Jordan, in January 1953 galvanized Israel's military leaders to adopt a different approach. In August 1953 they resurrected Wingate's ideas, forming Unit 101, an elite group named for the "Screaming Eagles" of the United States 101st Airborne Division.

Ariel Sharon, a precocious fighter who had recently left military life for academic pursuits, gained responsibility for assembling this formation, if such a term applies to men who deliberately flouted military customs and courtesies such as salutes and uniforms. Several recruits displayed eccentricities of one form or another, but Sharon transformed these quirks into potent military capabilities. Meir Har-Zion, not yet 20 when he joined Unit 101, is a good example. Har-Zion spent much of his youth exploring the Israeli countryside; these sojourns provided excellent training for his subsequent career as Israel's most skillful commando.

Training near Jerusalem, the irregulars of Unit 101 practiced demolition, long-range patrolling, and other techniques for seizing the initiative despite small numbers and limited firepower. Israel's small population relative to that of its neighbors and its culture of placing extraordinary value on the life of each Israeli soldier precluded the commandos from engaging in attritional warfare, thus limiting their tactical options and forcing Sharon always to consider potential casualties when planning raids.

Israel's experiment in special operations at first failed. The unit killed Arab soldiers and civilians alike in disregard for the traditional conventions of war, culminating in a non-combatant massacre at Kibya, Jordan. Israeli leaders reacted by changing Unit 101. Dayan combined the group with a paratroop unit, forming the 202nd Battalion in 1954. He apparently hoped to leaven 101's roguish spirit with a dose of discipline, at least regarding the laws of war. Conversely, he sought to inculcate the remainder of the IDF – these paratroops being his test case – with special operations tactical skills. Additionally, the Israeli general staff ordered Sharon to focus on military targets.

This he did, commencing a nearly three-year span during which the 202nd Battalion (and later the 202nd Brigade) conveyed through violence a message to Arab governments: Israel will punish your security forces if they fail to control borders. Assaulting targets such as police posts and military barracks posed special challenges for Israeli commandos. Concealed behind a trench-and-wire labyrinth and minefields, policemen and soldiers at these positions enjoyed the advantages accruing to defenders, and often had heavy-weapons support and reinforcements nearby.

Sharon surmounted these difficulties by assessing his adversary's combat tendencies. Since Arab armies made little effort to develop individual initiative among lower ranks, soldiers invariably floundered without strong leadership. Moreover, surprise often elicited reflexive reactions in Arab commanders, who typically dispatched help before assessing the situation. Like Wingate, Sharon noted that darkness attenuated firepower's role as a force multiplier. At night the killing range of modern weapons shrank by orders of magnitude, regressing combat to conditions prevalent centuries earlier.

The 202nd Battalion therefore implemented several exploitative tactics. Commandos always operated at night, and enhanced the element of surprise by firing only upon discovery. Their objective was to approach strongpoints within extremely

close range before Arab sentries detected them. At the moment of confrontation, Israeli troops immediately struck into the heart of enemy defenses. This concept was at variance with standard offensive tactics for storming fortified positions: spiraling concentrically through trenches from their periphery inward, methodically neutralizing resistance en route.

Firing short, aimed bursts from their standard-issue Uzi sub-machine guns, the commandos sprinted inwards, engulfing the command center in a deadly crossfire. Destroying a fortification's leaders typically paralyzed the entire garrison, who either milled about in a daze, making them easy targets or, better yet, cowered in their trenches. Such behavior made the commandos' next activity – demolishing every structure in and around the strongpoint – much easier. Through this phase of battle, both sides had often suffered only light casualties. However, Sharon then unveiled his pièce de résistance: a well-placed ambush, transforming a skirmish into all-out slaughter.

Commotion associated with buildings collapsing and large quantities of TNT exploding drew into the fray Arab assistance from nearby posts and villages. In the 202nd Battalion's early years, these reinforcements invariably blundered towards battle with little foresight and even less planning. Israeli gunmen waited along their path. Intelligence gleaned from prior nocturnal reconnaissance indicated which terrain along likely support routes provided optimal ambush conditions.

Taking cues from Hannibal at Lake Trasimene and Frederick the Great at Rossbach, the commandos preferred to set traps atop hills or other commanding heights bounding narrow axes of movement. While some detachments moved against the raid's primary objective, other Israeli commandos deployed on both sides of an ambush zone along the length of the confined area. Such arrangements provided formidable strength to the ambushers. After depleting their supply of grenades and ammunition on hapless soldiers below, the ambushing force withdrew to

Israel, heavy enemy casualties and wrecked fortifications in their wake.

Sharon's reprisal tactics exceeded his expectations even during experimentation in 1954, when nine major raids in Jordan and Syria humiliated those governments by demonstrating that they were incapable of defending their own territory. This impressive debut was merely a prelude to even greater success the following year. Israeli paratroops added Nasser to their list of psychological victims. Their February raid against northern Gaza, which smashed local authority while killing dozens of Egyptian police and soldiers, darkened Nasser's mood to a point where he embarked on a ruthless cycle of violence with his eastern neighbor.

Equally influential regarding regional and global politics was Israel's attack against Syria in December 1955. In keeping with Sharon's modus operandi, three groups of Israeli commandos operating at night struck strongpoints along the Sea of Galilee's eastern shore. Four other detachments simultaneously set ambushes along anticipated Syrian reinforcement routes. The extensive mayhem Sharon's paratroops inflicted on Syria elicited stern condemnation from the United Nations and a good portion of the world community as well.

By 1956, however, rising paratroop casualty rates portended the end of raids in which commandos operated with impunity deep inside enemy territory. Nietzsche noted that war makes the victor stupid. As the Middle East slipped towards general conflict in the mid-1950s, his observation gained a corollary: war enlightens the defeated. An October 1956

Israeli assault near Kalkiliya, Jordan, is instructive.

Here the 202nd Brigade launched a major raid against Arab Legion fortifications. Sharon, by now a servant of repetitive tactics, proceeded in his usual fashion: attack, dynamite, ambush, withdraw. Attacking and dynamiting proceeded according to plan. But commandos setting a trap for Jordanian reinforcements soon found themselves ambushed. After probing and locating Israeli blocking positions, troops of the Arab Legion turned their adversary's flank, cutting withdrawal routes to Israel. Only by resorting to massive artillery and air support did Sharon extricate his paratroops from their predicament, and not before losing 17 of Israel's best commandos. It was obvious to Israeli military commanders that tactics that had earlier kept Israeli casualties to a minimum now provided no such protection.

The 202nd Brigade was still licking its wounds from Kalkiliya and earlier setbacks at Husan and elsewhere in Jordan when the Sinai campaign began. Perhaps recognizing their ragged state, Dayan deployed the paratroops to a front where he expected only light resistance. Such was the irony of Kadesh – when outright war finally exploded late in 1956, those soldiers who for so long had functioned as Israel's spearhead and had borne the brunt of its shadow war against hostile forces now played a supporting role to reserve units. Moreover the bulk of the 202nd Brigade's casualties occurred at Heitan Defile, where Sharon, pursuing a useless objective, ignored the tactics that made his commandos so effective in the first place.

Britain and France abandon Revise

Poor Allied leadership at Port Said results in lost opportunities

Various miscommunications plagued the allies during their invasion. Soon after 45 Commando suffered friendly fire in northern Port Said, Stockwell and Beaufre learned of Egyptian interest in negotiating. They left their command ship *Tyne* aboard an amphibian, which, for unclear reasons, ferried them well south of friendly lines, to the Suez Canal Company offices. As bullets cracked around his head, Beaufre correctly concluded that surrender rumors were premature. Their amphibian retreated to the Fishing Harbor, where Stockwell subsequently debarked. He wandered around Port Said until well after nightfall. His decision to spend the day incommunicado rather than on board the *Tyne*, where updates from his superiors and situation reports were available, remains inexplicable. Beaufre made a similarly unfathomable choice. He lingered in the French zone, talking to French commanders at Port Fuad and preparing for subsequent Canal Zone operations.

Had the Task Force commander and his deputy been aboard the *Tyne* rather than engaged in courageous though aimless peregrinations, they would have learned of dramatic political developments. While 3 Commando Brigade picked through Port Said's maze of snipers and strongpoints, Eden conceded to intense domestic, American, and United Nations pressure. British ministers chose to accept a ceasefire, effective at 02:00 am local time on 7 November. Early in the afternoon of 6 November, they alerted allied HQ at Cyprus, and a few hours later directed Keightley to halt offensive operations soon.

One hundred miles south, Stockwell and Beaufre, unaware that planning for future operations had become a mere academic exercise, convened a mid-afternoon conference of senior leaders. During this summit, they arranged for al-Qantarah and al-Ismailiyah airborne landings on 7 November. French forces were to parachute into the former at dawn, while British airborne troops assaulted the latter a few hours later.

Forces capable of capturing these cities before the ceasefire took effect were in fact available in Port Said. In addition to 2 RPC at Raswa, French forces on the ground included three commando units, an AMX tank squadron, and the Ier Regiment Etranger Parachutiste. The latter, after landing on the morning of 5 November, consolidated French control of Port Fuad and destroyed pockets of Egyptian resistance at a police post east of town, inflicting nearly 100 casualties. 45 Commando was also available to participate in a southern advance. All afternoon these marines moved west – rather than south towards the important objectives – clearing snipers from the notoriously dangerous native quarter and seeking to rendezvous with 3 Para. This task had little value beyond a narrow tactical one.

Revise's overriding strategic aim was to advance to al-Qantarah, not to secure each and every building in Port Said. A few units – perhaps a troop or two – could have cordoned off the native quarter by establishing roadblocks at key junctions, while the majority of 45 Commando screened allied armor south of Raswa, available in abundance by late afternoon on 6 November. A Squadron, 6 RTR, having survived the treacherous terrain at Port Said's golf course, joined 2 RPC and 42 Commando at Raswa Bridge in mid-afternoon. B Squadron and regimental headquarters, both of which landed via LST at the Casino Palace Hotel,

French marines churn ashore unopposed at Port Fuad 6 November 1956. French paratroops captured this city a day earlier. (Topham Picturepoint)

also advanced to Raswa, arriving some hours after A Squadron. Since none at Raswa understood time's fleeting nature in light of the imminent ceasefire, break-out operations proceeded slowly. A Squadron's Centurions and 2 RPC paratroops began a leisurely advance along the al-Qantarah road, requiring a few hours to cover 16km (10 miles).

By nightfall these units reached al-Tinah, a small Canal station. In line with standard procedures, Lieutenant Colonel T.H. Gibbon, A Squadron commander, halted his column and established defensive positions. Gibbon, rightly reluctant to advance his armor at night without an infantry screen, did not know that thousands of troops capable of supporting such an offensive now occupied Port Said. Among these units were the 1st and 2nd Battalions of the 16th Parachute

Brigade, which debarked from their LSTs at the Casino Palace Hotel wharf. Nor did Gibbon receive orders to continue his southern advance. Neither Stockwell nor Beaufre was in a position to issue such orders, since both remained ashore, unaware of the pending ceasefire.

While Gibbon and his men entrenched south of Port Said at al-Tinah, the lead elements of 45 Commando and 3 Para west of the city were separated. Déjà vu comprised the dominant motif for these airborne forces on 6 November. They again struggled to overrun strongpoints they had occupied, but then abandoned, a day earlier. Staging from their sewage farm bivouac, the paratroops stormed the cemetery and coast guard barracks, occupying both areas without much difficulty before noon. East of the barracks, their progress slowed. Here the coastal road split, one prong heading north to Sierra Red and Green, the assault beaches north of Port Said, while the other branch veered south to the native quarter. Situated at this fork were several obstacles, including a medical complex and a police station. In these buildings the Egyptians used superior cover and advantageous fields of fire to mount a spirited defense, thus preventing 3 Para from continuing towards Port Said.

Air support, so useful in annihilating other Egyptian fortifications, again comprised the Royal Marines' preferred instrument. However, intense air operations elsewhere in the city prevented the RAF and Fleet Air Arm from striking the coastal road buildings with immediate and overwhelming force. Similar interruptions continued throughout the afternoon, again delaying 3 Para's advance. The increased danger and difficulty of night operations against a shadowy partisan foe postponed their rendezvous with 45 Commando until the following morning, 7 November, after the ceasefire took effect.

A British Centurion amidst devastation in Port Said. During Revise, Egyptian partisans fought from in large masonry buildings such as the structure on the left, slowing the British and French advance. (TRH Pictures)

Centurions lunge for al-Qantarah and establish a defensive perimeter

Halting at al-Tinah on the evening of 6 November apparently stopped the progress of A Squadron, 6 RTR, the British unit nearest al-Qantarah, until daybreak. Gibbon and his Centurions expected to bivouac at least through the night in defensive positions there. When Stockwell returned to the *Tyne* at approximately 09:00 pm that evening, however, he learned of the ceasefire that would take effect in five hours. He therefore ordered Gibbon to advance on al-Qantarah immediately. Four hours elapsed before British troops began traveling south in a chaotic procession.

Some units of the 2nd Parachute Battalion Group (2 Para) clambored onto 6 RTR Centurions, forming the vanguard of this advance; behind were engineers aboard other tanks. Trailing the armored column on foot was the rest of 2 Para. Darkness and craters along the Canal causeway, together with the

confusion caused by mixed units executing an ad hoc operation, combined to prevent the motley British formation from reaching al-Qantarah by 02:00 am on 7 November. Instead, that early hour found the lead Centurions and paratroop passengers at al-Cap, a Canal station four miles north of their objective and 40 km (25 miles) south of Port Said. Here British paratroops entrenched in darkness, with a small contingent – two platoons – protecting their narrow front line. Further back were Centurions of A Squadron. Once Egyptian forces in al-Qantarah learned that Britain and France had halted their advance and intended to respect the ceasefire, they established blocking positions between al-Cap and al-Qantarah, less than half a mile from British front lines.

With Revise now over, British and French forces faced two challenges. First, they needed to defend their al-Cap positions; second, they hoped to maintain control in Port Said, where civil authority had disappeared. Protecting al-Cap began in the early morning darkness of 7 November, and expanded once daylight illuminated the Canal Zone. British armor and anti-tank weapons assumed positions to fend off large-scale Egyptian attack. For nearly five days, 2 Para and 6 RTR defended the southern perimeter, enduring sporadic, mostly annoying small-arms fire and the uncertainty that Egypt might attack their positions at any time. Their replacements came primarily from the 29th Brigade, 3rd Infantry Division, which left Britain via troopship during Revise Phase I. The 1st Battalion Royal West Kents arrived at al-Cap on 11 November and served a 10-day stint in defense of British positions at al-Cap, at which point the Royal Fusiliers, then 1st Battalion, York and Lancaster Regiment, protected the al-Cap front line at roughly one-week intervals.

Responsibility for Port Said patrols fell mainly onto another brigade of the 3rd Infantry Division, the 19th. Port Said posed higher risk than al-Cap because its buildings and large population offered endless hiding places and a willing pool of potential snipers. Port Said's most dangerous district

After United Nations Emergency Force troops entered Egypt in late 1956, Britain and France withdrew all forces from the Canal Zone. Here, British paratroops await their departure from Port Said. (Topham Picturepoint)

A contingent of United Nations peacekeepers, including these Yugoslav soldiers, occupied Sinai in the aftermath of the Suez Crisis. (Topham Picturepoint)

was the native quarter in the northwest, which 45 Commando had partially subdued on 6 and 7 November as Revise came to a close. However, many partisans hostile to Britain and France remained, biding their time to fire upon exposed soldiers. After 3 Para and 45 Commando rotated from Port Said's front lines, the Royal Scots stepped into the native quarter breach. Less dangerous but hazardous nonetheless was patrol duty in Port Said's other districts; the Argyll and Sutherland Highlanders and the West Yorkshire Regiment shouldered responsibility for this task.

Peacekeepers into the Canal Zone and Sinai

For two weeks after the ceasefire, British and French forces attempted to maintain order and their positions in occupied Egyptian territory while awaiting the arrival of the United Nations Emergency Force (UNEF).

UNEF, a group of international peacekeepers, sprang from Canadian foreign minister Lester Pearson's early-November proposals. Attempting to buy time, Eden agreed to the presence of UNEF in Egypt, hoping that bureaucratic intricacies would delay its creation until after Revise ended and Britain and France had accomplished all their goals. He underestimated the momentum propelling UNEF, which a UN General Assembly resolution brought into existence on 5 November.

Two days later, another resolution barred British and French troops from participating in UNEF. After contentious debate regarding the composition of this force, UN resolutions allocated to Denmark and Norway responsibility for replacing British and French troops along the occupied territory of the northern Canal Zone. Approximately 200

Danes and an equal number of Norwegians separated the combatants in late November, the former deployed at al-Cap and the latter patrolling Port Said and Port Fuad. By December, hostile forces remained in contact along only one seam in Egypt: the Canal Zone south of al-Cap. On this axis, Israeli troops along the Canal's east bank faced Egyptians along its west bank. To a greater degree than his British and French partners, Ben-Gurion dug in his heels regarding withdrawal from territory captured during the Suez–Sinai War.

Whereas France and Britain viewed their Canal Zone occupation as an expendable bargaining chip, Ben-Gurion saw Sinai as a buffer shielding his nation from Arab attacks. Therefore he resisted mightily international efforts to expel Israeli forces from Sinai and place peacekeepers along the 1949 armistice line. Eventually he relented, although only after securing UN and American commitments to ensure freedom of navigation in the Tiran Straits. In March 1957, Israel completed its withdrawal from Sinai, and UNEF took up positions between the belligerents. From a territorial standpoint at least, the status quo ante bellum now prevailed, four months after Kadesh sent thousands of Israeli forces into Sinai.

Political ramifications of the ceasefire and subsequent withdrawal

The 7 November ceasefire showed that Revise had failed. Britain and France did not topple Nasser, nor did they seize the Canal Zone. Their forces controlled Port Said and Port Fuad and the northern sector of the Canal Zone, and they initially hoped to maintain this occupation as a bargaining chip in negotiating the Canal's future. But world events undercut their plan. Heavy American political and economic pressure against both countries, targeting in particular Britain's

financial weakness, was particularly telling. In Britain, currency reserves plummeted during early November, accelerating a trend that threatened profound economic damage.

Exacerbating this grave situation was an oil crisis in Britain. Canal blockages forced tankers carrying crude from the Arabian Peninsula to steam around Africa instead,

French paratroops who had attacked Port Said on 5 November withdraw from Egypt, December 1956. (Topham Picturepoint)

an expensive and time-consuming diversion. Destruction of regional pipelines in Syria further constricted the flow of oil to Europe. Consumption soon exceeded supply, causing widespread economic dislocation in Britain. Rationing alleviated these shortages to some extent, but carried an obvious political price.

By mid-November Eden's stamina collapsed. Balancing the conflicting demands of his cabinet, the Labour Party, the United States, and the UN proved more than his body could tolerate, and he therefore decided to convalesce for a month in Jamaica. During his absence the cabinet, with Lord Privy Seal R.A.B. Butler and

Chancellor of the Exchequer Harold Macmillan in the lead, chose to withdraw unconditionally from Egypt in return for American aid to save Britain's faltering economy. The cabinet's decision came on 3 December. By this time, Eden was a mere figurehead, as events soon showed. Upon his mid-December return, he retained power for only a few weeks. In early January 1957, Macmillan became prime minister, and Eden's three-decade political career was over.

Whereas Macmillan decided to reinvigorate ties with the United States after the Suez Crisis, France came to a different decision, concluding that neither Britain nor the United States was a genuine ally. After all, Britain wavered during the war's climactic moments and the United States obstructed French efforts to occupy the Canal Zone and overthrow Nasser. France therefore parted from its NATO colleagues, pursuing an independent path that included the development of its own nuclear force.

Charles De Gaulle led this shift in French policy. After a long period in the political wilderness, Revise and its resulting political and military strife within France propelled him into a leadership role. Despite confidence and belief in his own destiny, De Gaulle failed to stem an anti-colonial tide of which the Suez Crisis was just one manifestation. During the Cold War, French colonies in Africa and elsewhere gained independence in droves. Algeria, which prompted French interest in toppling Nasser, left the French fold five years after the Suez Crisis.

Israel learned from the Suez Crisis similar lessons to those of France. For instance, Israeli leaders decided that the capacity for independent action was paramount for survival. Depending on other states for direct military assistance – such as destroying Egyptian bombers – was too risky, because those states might renege on their commitments. The Suez War also reinforced Israeli tendencies towards striking first. By keeping Egyptian forces off-balance and confused, this approach worked in Kadesh, and Israel applied these lessons 11 years later during the Six-Day War.

Surprisingly, Nasser emerged from the Suez Crisis a hero both in Egypt and abroad. Although Egyptian forces fought with mediocre skill during the conflict, many Arabs saw Nasser as the conqueror of European colonialism and Zionism, simply because Britain, France, and Israel left Sinai and the northern Canal Zone. In 1958, Nasser took a dramatic step towards his pan-Arab vision by linking Egypt and Syria in the United Arab Republic. Pro-Nasser factions elsewhere in the Middle East, such as Iraq, attempted to emulate his ideas by overthrowing the status quo leadership.

Nasser's new-found stature as a leader of world importance lasted about a decade. Egypt's crushing 1967 defeat diminished his stature considerably, and probably contributed to his death at the age of 53 in 1970. The United Arab Republic proved a disappointment, and at the turn of the millennium pan-Arabism lay in tatters, the Islamist movement having replaced it as the Arab world's most dynamic force.

Destruction in Egypt and Gaza

Most wars affect civilians. The Suez Crisis was no exception, but its impact was one-sided. Apart from the inconvenience of fuel rationing, this conflict barely touched the home front in Britain or France. Widespread mobilization disrupted daily life in Israel, but its civilians suffered neither casualties nor property damage. Communities in Egypt and Egyptian-controlled Gaza, by contrast, bore the brunt of the war. Fighting raged in their houses, schools, and markets, leaving death and destruction in its wake.

For those in Gaza, the Suez Crisis was the latest in a string of misfortunes dating back to the 1948–49 Arab–Israeli War. That conflict, which accompanied Israel's creation, forced hundreds of thousands of Palestinians to flee their homes. Many refugees sought shelter in Gaza. Formerly under British Mandatory authority, after the 1948–49 war Egypt administered this territory.

Most refugees, including those inundating Gaza, expected to return to their homes at

Eden attempted to minimize the destruction Revise inflicted on Egypt, but bombing and artillery fire resulted in much collateral damage such as Port Said's Abbas Street, pictured here. (Topham Picturepoint)

war's end. Events proved otherwise. To make matters worse, Egypt granted neither self-determination nor citizenship to these displaced newcomers, who lived as subject peoples with few political rights. Furthermore Gaza's infrastructure was completely inadequate to support such a large population. Egypt, which wanted the refugees to return home, had little incentive to improve living conditions in the Gaza camps. Nor did the Palestinians themselves want to expend time and energy developing accommodation they expected to be temporary. The UN, recognizing this humanitarian disaster, formed the Relief and Works Agency for Palestinian Refugees (UNRWA) in 1949. UNRWA improved life in Gaza somewhat, but conditions deteriorated when Egypt began attacking Israel from Gaza. Predictably, its inhabitants were caught amidst escalating conflict as Egypt and Israel launched raids and counter-raids against one another.

Such violence helped push Israel and Egypt to war in 1956. That November the IDF

Israeli forces withdraw from Sinai after a four-month occupation, March 1957. (Topham Picturepoint)

attacked Gaza. Several battles erupted in its cities, particularly at Khan Yunus and Gaza City. Incomplete records render a precise accounting of civilian casualties difficult; a reasonable estimate is that the fighting killed or wounded dozens, perhaps hundreds, of non-combatants. The indiscriminate firepower accompanying modern urban warfare made such casualties almost inevitable, despite Israel's decision not to target civilians. This tally also neglects the psychological strain associated with nearby combat. For civilians, death or injury could materialize out of the blue at any time while fighting continued in Gaza.

Also disruptive was the upheaval accompanying the Israeli invasion of Gaza. Some Palestinians ransacked UNRWA warehouses, complicating food and medicine distribution to needy refugees. While holding Gaza for nearly five months, moreover, Israel, like Egypt before it, governed the territory as a police state. Israel would not countenance Palestinian autonomy, leaving Gazans to chafe in oppressive conditions. Nor did Israel improve living conditions, and the refugees continued to languish in primitive camps.

With Palestinian nationalism in its nascent stages – maturation remained a few decades away – resistance to Israeli occupation was disorganized and sporadic. But the humiliation and despair associated with Israel's conquest of Gaza planted seeds among Palestinians that later resulted in anti-Israeli sentiment along with widespread support for unlimited statehood. Israel contributed to these explosive trends by devastating territory it occupied during the Suez Crisis. Israel's stated pretext for destroying most infrastructure before withdrawing from occupied land in March 1957 was to prevent its future use as a staging area for Arab attacks. To many, however, this destruction appeared to have no basis other than spite.

The Suez Crisis affected civilians in Gaza, but Egypt suffered even greater destruction. Not only did fierce fighting rage throughout Port Said and elsewhere, but non-combatants also became unwilling pawns in a larger political struggle. Nasser, Britain, and France all used civilians to advance their own ends, placing the Egyptian populace directly at risk. Nasser saw Egypt's civilians as the basis

People's war: the aftermath. Egyptian leaders dispersed thousands of weapons, including those pictured here in British custody, among civilians in the Canal Zone with instructions to use them against enemy soldiers. (TRH Pictures)

for a popular insurgency against European colonialism, while Britain and France saw that group as the basis for a popular insurgency against Nasser. Whereas Nasser's ploy succeeded to some extent, the British and French plan for civilian exploitation collapsed in utter failure.

Nasser saw Egyptian civilians as a weapon of last resort. Although he preferred using properly trained and equipped military forces, if circumstances deteriorated he planned to transform non-combatants into combatants. In this scenario, Egypt would wage a "people's war" against invaders. Troops were to jettison all military trappings – uniforms and the like – except their weapons, and disperse incognito into the population. They would then lead civilians in resisting Anglo-French occupation.

For Nasser, the advantage of a "people's war" was its obliteration of lines demarcating military and civilian spheres. With this distinction blurred, British and French soldiers faced dilemmas: who is our enemy, and under what circumstances are we to use deadly force? Nasser understood the delicate political nature of allied operations in Egypt and the intense public scrutiny they entailed; these conditions exacerbated for Britain and France thorny questions regarding proper rules of engagement.

If British and French troops aggressively countered the popular insurgency, many civilians, even those not involved in the "people's war," would die. High civilian casualties would increase pressure in Britain, France, and abroad to cease hostilities and withdraw from Egypt. Moreover, such casualties would persuade more Egyptians to resist occupation, again expanding the conflict in Egypt's favor.

Alternatively, if Britain and France cautiously countered the "people's war," Egyptian partisans could attack with near impunity by hiding among crowds of apparent non-combatants. The resulting British and French casualties might provide the impetus for those countries to abandon Egypt. Essentially Nasser hoped to replicate in microcosm the asymmetric strategy of the Algerian revolution, still in its preliminary phase at the time of the Suez Crisis, but nonetheless showing promise as a way for a militarily inferior state to vanquish its more powerful adversary.

When British and French warplanes attacked Egypt on 31 October, 1956, Nasser implemented this philosophy. Realizing that an invasion was imminent, he directed all Egyptians, soldiers and civilians, to resist Britain and France. Expecting those nations to attack Port Said, he distributed assault rifles and grenades, instructing recipients to use them to harass occupying forces at every opportunity.

Most Egyptian civilians were unfamiliar with sophisticated military technology, limiting somewhat their effectiveness as partisans. However, civilians could easily master basic munitions such as grenades. On 5 November several weapons shipments arrived via rail in Port Said; pallets of grenades, Czech assault rifles, and other devices were available on street corners, offered to anyone hoping to resist the imminent invasion.

Probably just a small percentage of Port Said's civilians participated in hostilities. Nonetheless their "people's war" had significance. Relentless sniping forced Royal Marines to seek armored protection when moving along city streets, hindering their advance. Armed civilians concealed themselves inside Port Said's buildings; the threat they posed slowed the progress of soldiers engaged in clearing operations. These delays prevented a rapid allied break-out from Port Said. When the 7 November UN ceasefire took effect, British and French troops had not reached al-Qantarah, the next city south of Port Said. After the ceasefire, Egyptian insurgents continued resisting occupation. They sniped and threw grenades at patrolling soldiers, inflicting a few casualties at a time and providing an additional incentive for Britain and France to leave Egypt.

For Nasser, the Egyptian people had an unambiguous role: resist invading forces, delay their advance, and swing world opinion into line behind Egypt. In Anglo-French strategy, by contrast, Egyptian civilians constituted a paradox. In some ways, the allies, especially the British, sought to minimize the suffering of the Egyptian people. Indeed, concern over potential non-combatant casualties forced Eden to abandon Alexandria as a bridgehead for invasion. While planning the Egyptian campaign, Mountbatten and other British leaders fretted that attacking cities would stigmatize them as "murderers and baby killers" and injure Britain internationally. During Revise Phase I, in which bombers struck airfields, Eden repeatedly modified target lists to avoid hitting civilians. Just before British and French forces stormed Port Said, the cabinet limited bomb and gun size for aerial and naval bombardment despite their knowledge that such restrictions might increase British losses. Although some military commanders disregarded these stipulations, the restrictions illustrate palpable British concern

– political, moral, or otherwise – at the highest levels for non-combatant safety.

Yet the very success of Revise rested on terrorizing Egypt's civilian population. Phase II, which Keightley hoped would form the crux of allied military operations by forcing a regime change in Egypt, attempted to coerce Egyptians through a bombing offensive. RAF planners who designed the "aero-psychological" campaign had full confidence that disrupting daily life would compel Egypt's people to topple Nasser. Air strikes against communications and transportation networks were to be the mechanism for paralyzing Egyptian society.

Perhaps recognizing the contradictions in British strategy, and at last understanding the political repercussions of a terror bombing campaign, Eden eliminated many of Phase II's more aggressive tactics. Aircrew resistance and technical challenges undercut other aspects of the aerial offensive. However, many bombs still fell on Egypt, inflicting scores, perhaps hundreds, of civilian casualties in Cairo and adjoining areas. British pilots, operating unfamiliar weapons systems and steeped in an "area bombing"

French soldiers in bush hats placing a mine along a barbed wire fence in Algeria. (Topham Picturepoint)

culture rather than in precision tactics, often placed ordnance on unintended targets, killing or wounding non-combatants. International pressure and an awareness that Phase II served to rally, not destroy, Egyptian morale led Keightley to cancel Phase II soon after its awkward inception.

Port Said, unlike Cairo, escaped the ravages of Revise Phase II, but bore the full weight of Phase III. As fighting shifted there on 5 November, its residents, even those who demurred from the "people's war" against invading troops, found themselves in the crossfire of a ferocious two-day battle. Especially vulnerable was Port Said's native quarter. Wood shanties fed fires resulting from artillery and air strikes. Strong winds began the afternoon of 5 November and persisted throughout 6 November, fanning the flames that eventually burned down much of the native quarter. As tens of thousands of Egyptians lived in this area, the conflagration left many homeless.

Port Said's civilians absorbed another blow on the morning of 5 November when French paratroops captured the municipal waterworks, severing the city's water source. For the next 12 hours, water remained inaccessible, impeding food preparation and other aspects of daily life. How long the allies intended to strangle Port Said by denying its residents water is unclear; during negotiations on the evening of 5 November, British and French commanders agreed to restore the water supply.

D-Day, 6 November, intensified the combat in Port Said. Entire blocks, particularly those along the waterfront and beaches, succumbed to air strikes, artillery, and naval shelling. Throughout the city,

flying debris filled the air. Civilians wishing to avoid injury or death from this deadly mist had two choices: stay indoors while hoping no shells landed on top of one's shelter, or evacuate the city. Understandably, many chose to flee, especially those left destitute from fires consuming the native quarter and other areas, but they had nowhere to go and, even if they did have a destination, no way to travel except on foot. Groups found themselves milling around southern Port Said since that sector seemed the least dangerous.

Another detriment to civilian life in the city arose out of its isolation during and after Revise Phase III. Port Said, with its hundreds of thousands of residents, depended on outside provisions for survival. On D-Day this supply network collapsed, with most metropolitan roads impassable and the Canal and harbor closed. For three weeks, civilians in Port Said lived hand-to-mouth. Having no organized relief plan, Britain attempted some scattershot assistance to limited effect. As grocers exhausted their inventories, many inhabitants scraped by on starvation rations. UNEF's late November arrival somewhat eased the city's supply crisis, although the return to normal life occurred only when the Canal reopened in April 1957.

Taken in its entirety, the Suez Crisis inflicted profound hardship on Arab civilians. Although Britain, France, and Israel hoped to avoid this outcome, such devastation was predictable. Combat in populated areas invariably leads to widespread destruction, and civilians usually have neither the means nor the ability to protect themselves during the fluid urban battles that characterized this form of war.

A transitional conflict

As 20th-century conflicts go, the Suez Crisis was temporally and geographically limited, lasting a little over one week and confined to northern Egypt. With the exception of Egypt, casualties were light: 189 Israeli, 16 British, and 10 French dead. Egyptian losses have never been precisely tabulated, but consisted of approximately 1000 civilian and 1650 military (650 at Port Said and Port Fuad and the balance in Sinai) deaths.

Despite its limited scale, the Suez Crisis indicates the evolution of military affairs, representing a transition between World War II and more technologically intense conflicts of the Cold War and beyond. Particularly important is its role as a bellwether predicting future Middle Eastern styles of combat. Desert landscapes allowed a higher degree of mobility than that attainable elsewhere, and air power flourished in a setting where ground targets had few hiding places. This pattern of extreme mobility and air power dominance reached a climax in Desert Storm, but had its roots in central Sinai, where in 1956 armored brigades teamed with Israeli warplanes to pursue and destroy Egyptian formations. Tanks outflanked Egyptian troops, forcing them to move or face encirclement. Once in motion the Egyptians suffered merciless Israeli air strikes.

Air power's magnified effectiveness in arid conditions is also evident in those situations where Egypt attempted to reinforce sectors facing Israeli attack. If they hoped to escape destruction, units moving to assist their countrymen could move only at night, and needed to find protective cover – sparse at best in Sinai – before dawn. To operate in the open during daylight meant heavy losses to Israeli strikes. Air power played such a crucial role in the Suez Crisis that a short analysis is appropriate. Transportation, reconnaissance, close air support, interdiction and strategic bombing all influenced the war. Probably the most successful aerial mission was the airlift. Paratroop and helicopter operations at Mitla, Gamil, Raswa, Port Said, and Port Fuad all achieved tactical objectives, although in Telescope Modified constraints on airfield space prevented unlimited success. Given the ineffectiveness of Revise Phase II strategic bombing, basing additional Hastings and Valettas in Cyprus would have benefited Anglo-French efforts. Helicopter assault showed promise as a technique for transporting troops into small landing zones. British success in ferrying 45 Commando to Port Said prefigures extensive use of rotary-wing aircraft in conflicts such as Southeast Asia and Afghanistan – a staple of modern warfare.

Close air support and interdiction also succeeded to a significant degree. At Raswa on 5 November, for instance, French aircraft annihilated Egyptian forces attempting to engage British and French paratroops. Also on that day, Israeli fighter-bomber attacks at Sharm el-Sheikh's fortifications brought Yotvat – and Kadesh – to successful conclusions. Without this aerial support, Israeli ground forces may have required several more days to accomplish their objectives. The following day, Anglo-French air strikes at Port Said's Navy House and coast guard barracks enabled Royal Marines to advance along the harbor and establish landing areas for British ships. However, coordination and target identification challenges meant that close air support also frequently inflicted friendly casualties. This issue has plagued air forces since the dawn of air power, continues to do so decades after the Suez Crisis, and is probably inevitable during fluid engagements where friendly and enemy forces are in close contact. Interdiction sorties, while facing fewer of these challenges, were also susceptible to unwitting attacks on friendly troops. As in the case of close air support, fluid campaigns presented the highest risk of friendly fire. Nonetheless, interdiction assisted in limiting Egyptian reinforcement of Port Said and eastern Sinai, and hindered Egypt's general retreat towards the Canal Zone.

Strategic bombing was the least successful of the aerial missions. Revise Phase II and its aero-psychological ambitions proved an abject disappointment. Eden and Keightley bear responsibility for misjudging world opinion with respect to a strategic bombing campaign against Egypt. Eden's decision not to strike Radio Cairo shows that he had some inkling of the public relations implications of hitting targets in civilian areas, but he failed to grasp how the world might respond to the sight of British planes raining bombs on Cairo. Also, RAF weapons and skills were unsuited to the task at hand – disrupting the Egyptian economy and damaging morale while inflicting minimal civilian casualties. The RAF had no tradition of pinpoint bombing, and in an era before precision-guided munitions high-altitude night attacks against specific targets were quite difficult. Under these conditions, ordnance dispersed, as happened during Revise Phase I Canberra and Valiant raids on Egyptian airfields. In the end, relatively few bombs fell, and those that did mostly missed, leaving the Egyptian air force intact and Egyptian morale strong.

The Suez Crisis' role as a transitional conflict is all the more interesting in light of the fact that many concepts central to this war dated back decades or more. Dayan approached most objectives indirectly, emphasized mobility and creativity, and reinforced success. If Israeli troops attained a breakthrough, he exhorted them to exploit

their advantage with maximum speed. This philosophy echoes blitzkrieg, a style of fighting that European armies pioneered during the world wars. Another established form of conflict on display was urban warfare. While campaigning in the large population centers of Port Said and Port Fuad, British and French forces struggled to differentiate combatant from noncombatant. Egyptian irregulars could snipe with near impunity, and then melt into the surrounding civilian crowds until another opportunity presented itself. Hiding places abounded among the thousands of metropolitan buildings and homes. Germany had experienced similar difficulties at Stalingrad, and after the Suez Crisis comparable experiences would vex American and Israeli forces in cities such as Hue, Beirut, and Mogadishu. As Britain and France learned, no tidy solution exists to the urban warfare riddle. Fighting block by block means casualties, but also requires time and perseverance. The hectic pace of Telescope Modified and Revise Phase III made few allowances for these factors.

In general, the Suez Crisis' outcome exemplifies the connections linking politics and conflict. British and French leaders recognized the synergy of these elements – hence their decisions to delay war until exploring peaceful options, and to use Israel as a stalking-horse for their own ambitions – but at last failed to understand that military action ran against prevailing sentiment among their allies and throughout the world. Therefore, when Britain and France initiated Revise on 31 October, they operated in a confined political space. These restrictions soon forced military action to cease, leaving British and French objectives unrealized.

Further reading

Barker, A.J., *Suez: The Seven-Day War* (London, 1964)

Bar-On, Mordecai, *The Gates of Gaza: Israel's Road to Suez and Back* (New York, 1992)

Bar-Zohar, Michael, *Ben-Gurion: The Armed Prophet* (London, 1968)

Beaufre, Andre, *The Suez Expedition* (London, 1969)

Clark, D.M.J., *Suez Touchdown: A Soldier's Tale* (London, 1964)

Dayan, Moshe, *Diary of the Sinai Campaign* (London, 1967)

Dupuy, Trevor, *Elusive Victory: The Arab–Israeli Wars, 1947–1974* (New York, 1978)

Fullick, Roy and Powell, Geoffrey, *Suez: The Double War* (London, 1979)

Henriques, Robert, *A Hundred Hours to Suez: An Account of Israel's Campaign in the Sinai* (New York, 1957)

Katz, Samuel, *Soldier Spies: Israeli Military Intelligence* (Novato, CA, 1992)

Kyle, Keith, *Suez* (London, 1991)

Love, Kennett, *Suez: The Twice-Fought War* (London, 1970)

Lucas, Scott, *Britain and Suez: The Lion's Last Roar* (London, 1996)

Lucas, Scott, *Divided We Stand: Britain, the US, and the Suez Crisis* (London, 1996)

Luttwak, Edward and Dan Horowitz, *The Israeli Army* (New York, 1975)

Marshall, S.L.A., *Sinai Victory* (New York, 1958)

Neff, Donald, *Warriors at Suez* (New York, 1981)

Sharon, Ariel, *Warrior: An Autobiography* (London, 1989)

Van Creveld, Martin, *The Sword and the Olive* (New York, 1998)

Westwood, J.N., *The History of the Middle East Wars* (New York, 1986)

Index

Related titles from Osprey Publishing

To order any of these titles, or for more information on Osprey Publishing, contact:

Osprey Direct (UK) *Tel:* +44 (0)1933 443863 *Fax:* +44 (0)1933 443849 *E-mail:* info@ospreydirect.co.uk

Osprey Direct (USA) c/o MBI Publishing *Toll-free:* 1 800 826 6600 *Phone:* 1 715 294 3345

Fax: 1 715 294 4448 *E-mail:* info@ospreydirectusa.com

www.ospreypublishing.com

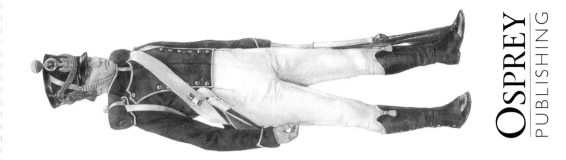

FIND OUT MORE ABOUT OSPREY

❏ Please send me a FREE trial issue of Osprey Military Journal

❏ Please send me the latest listing of Osprey's publications

❏ I would like to subscribe to Osprey's e-mail newsletter

Title/rank

Name

Address

Postcode/zip

State/country

E-mail

Which book did this card come from?

❏ I am interested in military history

My preferred period of military history is _____

❏ I am interested in military aviation

My preferred period of military aviation is _____

I am interested in (please tick all that apply)

❏ general history   ❏ militaria   ❏ model making

❏ wargaming   ❏ re-enactment

Please send to:

USA & Canada:
Osprey Direct USA, c/o MBI Publishing,
PO Box 1, 729 Prospect Ave, Osceola, WI 54020, USA

UK, Europe and rest of world:
Osprey Direct UK, PO Box 140, Wellingborough,
Northants, NN8 2FA, United Kingdom

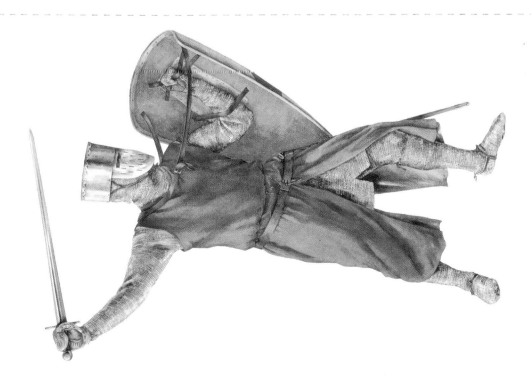

www.ospreypublishing.com

call our telephone hotline
for a free information pack

USA & Canada: 1-800-826-6600
UK, Europe and rest of world call:
+44 (0) 1933 443 863

Young Guardsman
Figure taken from *Warrior 22:
Imperial Guardsman 1799–1815*
Published by Osprey
Illustrated by Christa Hook

Knight, c.1190
Figure taken from *Warrior 1: Norman Knight 950 – 1204AD*
Published by Osprey
Illustrated by Christa Hook

POSTCARD